PENGUIN B(

Greek

BIBLE

Dear Ewa,

Kali Orexi

Greek

BIBLE

Lots of love

Yvonne Kaponis

17.10.10

Contents

Introduction

The essence of Greek cuisine is the use of seasonal, fresh ingredients. Dishes are designed to showcase the bounty of the season, the flavours of the meat and vegetables enhanced with fragrant herbs and spices, such as oregano, parsley, cinnamon and cloves.

Greek life is infused with many cultural and religious traditions. The preparation of dishes for the various annual celebrations brings the family together and these are occasions for sharing passion and fun – the customs around food almost as important as the events themselves.

Greek Basics

Many classic Greek dishes are connected to or have evolved as the result of the festivities held throughout the year. During lent, for example, orthodox Greeks refrain from eating meat and dairy, and favourite dishes eaten during that time include tomatoes stuffed with rice, *fasolada* (bean soup), baked potatoes, and dips. The fast is broken at midnight mass on Saturday and celebrated with a feast on Easter Sunday and on this day households will traditionally cook a whole lamb on the spit, accompanied by *moussaka*, *pastitsio*, salads and a plethora of other delicacies. Sweets such as *tsoureki* (Easter bread) and *koulouria* (Easter biscuits) will also be on hand.

Regional Influences

The cuisine of this ancient nation has of course been influenced by its rich and varied history. Several centuries before Christ, Alexander the Great extended the Greek Empire from Europe to India, then in 146 BC Greece fell to the Romans. About 500 years later Emperor

Constantine moved the capital of the Roman Empire to Constantinople, where the Byzantine empire was later founded. Constantinople fell to the Turks in 1453 and remained part of the Ottoman Empire for nearly 400 years. All of these eras have laid their stamp on the food of Greece – one example being that many Greek dishes still carry Turkish names.

There are more than ten geographic regions in Greece and each has its own unique cuisine, and specialty ingredients and dishes. Crete (the largest of the Greek islands), for example, is famous for its olives, olive oil, snails, cheeses, pastries and breads. It also exports fruits and vegetables to other parts of Greece and to northern Europe.

During the Golden Age of Greece (from around 500 to 300 BC), on the island of Kos, people were very conscious of their health and ate a well-balanced diet that included meat, fish, eggs, cereals, milk, cheese, fruits and vegetables. Foods were boiled or baked instead of fried, which later became a common way of preparing food. It was here that Hippocrates, one of the most influential and esteemed physicians in the history of medicine, uncovered the medicinal benefits of various herbs and plants – like chamomile, peppermint, sage and lemon – that could be used in cooking or drunk as teas.

The city of Thessaloniki, in the north, is known as the gastronomic capital of Greece. The narrow streets are filled with the aromas of *kritharaki* (risoni), *dolmades* (stuffed vine leaves), and the region's famous *bougatsa* (pastry filled with custard and cheese). Thessaloniki's pastry shops (*zaharoplastia*) offering a vast range of filo pastry sweets filled with nuts and dripping with honey syrup.

The small island of Kastellorizo is famous for its *strava* – sweet pastries filled with almonds and walnuts, and dipped in a honey–cinnamon syrup. Epirus, in north-western Greece, has a strong history of cheese production, the legacy of the nomadic shepherds who used to herd their flocks of sheep and goats to the plains of this region after grazing in the green grass of the mountains. Some of the best cheeses come from the municipality of Dodoni (the site of the ancient oracle Dodona).

Essential Ingredients

Greece is a nation of small farmers and there is an incredible array of produce available from the small street markets found in every town. The climate is perfect for growing olive and lemon trees, and both ingredients have been a staple part of the Greek diet for hundreds of years, along with fruits, fresh vegetable, pulses and cheeses (particularly those made from goat's milk). Greeks tend to eat more fish and poultry than red meat, though this has shifted somewhat in recent years as lamb and beef have become more readily available.

Around 80 percent of Greece is surrounded by the Mediterranean Sea, with 20 percent of the country made

up of islands – so it's no surprise that seafood features prominently in the Greek diet. *Psari plaki* (baked fish with tomato, onion and lemon), a dish from the island of Spetses, is just one of the many ways fish may be baked. In Mytilene (the capital of Lesbos) they serve char-grilled octopus as a meze with a shot of ouzo. Fisherman's soup made with the catch of the day is very popular through most of the Greek islands. The most important rule when purchasing seafood is to make sure it is absolutely fresh – look for clear eyes, a fresh salty smell (not fishy), and use it on the same day.

Fresh or dried **herbs** are used in almost every Greek dish. The most common are flat-leaf parsley, basil, mint, bay, rosemary, dill, fennel and oregano. **Spices** such as nutmeg, cinnamon and cloves also give Greek food its distinctive character. When purchasing dried herbs and spices, buy only small amounts and store them in an airtight container in a cool dark place to preserve their flavour.

Cheeses play an extremely important role in Greek cooking – whether crumbled into a salad, fried for a meze, or grated over a pasta dish. Different cheeses are suited to different uses, depending on their flavour and texture – for example, haloumi is a hard cheese with a high melting point, which makes it perfect for frying or grilling. Some of the most popular cheeses are: fetta, kasseri, kefalotiri, kefalograviera and haloumi (see Special Ingredients, page 248, for more information on particular cheeses).

Nuts are another important part of Greek cuisine, particularly almonds, walnuts, pistachios and pine nuts. Make sure you purchase fresh nuts, and store them in a sealed container in a cool dark place to maintain their flavour and texture.

The Greek Kitchen

The kitchen is where recipes are handed down through the generations. Grandmothers, mothers and daughters can be found making delicious meals together,

creating recipes to keep the family happily nourished with mouth-watering meals.

Family unity in the kitchen is especially important around Easter time. During the weeks leading up to Easter Sunday, the kitchen is a hotbed of activity with everyone helping to make a hearty feast, much needed after weeks of fasting. The most important dish is the lamb.

Early in the day, the coals of the spit are lit to make sure they are hot enough to cook the lamb. The lamb is then spit-roasted over charcoal (gas-fired spits are available but charcoal gives a nicer flavour) for many hours resulting in tender, mouth-watering pieces of meat.

A Greek kitchen can be successfully equipped with ingredients that are readily available from most supermarkets or delis. So get cooking and *kali orexi* (bon appétit)!

Meze

Greek cuisine is characterised by its simplicity and unadulterated natural flavours. To a large extent this can be seen in the large variety of meze (appetisers) – delicious dips, pastries, olives, sausages and stuffed vine leaves, to name a few.

These dishes are traditionally served with grilled pita or crusty bread, and accompanied with a nice cold glass of retsina, beer or ouzo.

Greeks rarely drink alcohol without eating – even a small glass of ouzo or wine is usually served with a small plate of meze.

< Helen's Dolmades (page 14)

Helen's Dolmades

Makes about 50

1 tablespoon (20 g/¾ oz) butter

2 tablespoons
(40 ml/1½ fl oz) oil

1 onion, finely chopped

500 g (1 lb 2 oz) lamb mince
(or beef mince)

1 × 400-g (14-oz) can chopped
tomatoes

1 tablespoon dried oregano

¼ teaspoon ground allspice

salt and freshly ground
black pepper

½ cup medium-grain rice

½ cup chopped fresh parsley

1 cup chopped fresh mint

250 g (9 oz) vine leaves
(see note)

½ cup (125 ml/4 fl oz) freshly
squeezed lemon juice,
plus extra to serve

1 cup (250 ml/8½ fl oz)
chicken stock

2 tablespoons (40 ml/1½ fl oz)
olive oil

tzatziki (page 37), to serve

Heat butter and oil in a frying pan over medium heat. Add onion and sauté until soft and caramelised. Add mince, reduce heat and stir until browned (about 10 minutes). Add tomatoes, dried oregano, allspice, and salt and pepper to taste. Simmer for 10 minutes.

Stir rice into the meat and tomato mixture. Add the parsley and mint, and simmer for another 5 minutes. Turn off heat and let cool.

On a clean surface, place a prepared vine leaf with the vein facing up and cut off the stem. Place a tablespoonful of the rice mixture at the bottom of the vine leaf. Fold over the bottom of the vine leaf, tuck in the sides and roll into a short cigar shape. Repeat with the remaining mixture.

Grease a heavy-based saucepan and line with baking paper. Cover the baking paper with any left-over, broken vine leaves. Arrange stuffed vine leaves in rows in the bottom of the saucepan and continue to layer (rows should all face the same way) until saucepan is three-quarters full.

Pour lemon juice and chicken stock over the dolmades and drizzle with olive oil. Place an overproof dinner plate on top of the vine leaves and press down gently – this helps the dolmades keep their shape. Simmer on low–medium heat for about 30–40 minutes until dolmades are tender.

Remove dolmades from the saucepan, squeeze with lemon juice and serve (hot or cold) with tzatziki.

🏛 Vine leaves can be purchased from any Greek deli. It is preferable to use brined leaves for this recipe. If using fresh leaves, blanch in boiling salted water for 5 minutes. Drain and let cool. If using bottled leaves, soak them in cold water for about ½ hour before use (this removes the saltiness). If the vine leaves are small, you may need to use two leaves (overlapped) for each dolmade.

Chickpea Patties

Revithopites

Makes about 50

500 g (1 lb 12 oz) chickpeas,
  soaked overnight in cold
  water

2 medium-sized onions

3 cloves garlic (optional)

800 g (1 lb 12 oz) canned
  chopped tomatoes

1 red capsicum, chopped

1 bunch fresh flat-leaf parsley

salt and freshly ground
  black pepper

½ teaspoon ground cumin

½ teaspoon ground coriander

1 teaspoon dried oregano

1 teaspoon bicarbonate of soda

1 × 400-g (14-oz) can
  creamed corn

1 cup (150 g/5 oz) plain flour

vegetable oil for shallow-
  frying

Put all ingredients (except creamed corn and flour) in a food processor, and process until well combined.

Place the mixture in a bowl and add creamed corn and flour and mix well. (If mixture is too sticky, add a little more flour.)

Heat 2.5 cm (1 in) oil in a heavy-based frying pan over moderate heat. Drop tablespoons of mixture into the oil and cook for 2–3 minutes, until golden-brown, then turn and cook the other side for a further 2–3 minutes. Remove patties and place on paper towel to drain. Serve hot or cold with tzatziki or hummus.

Marinated Olives

3 tablespoons (60 ml/2 fl oz)
olive oil

3 cloves garlic, thinly sliced

2 cups pitted kalamata olives

1 cup pitted green olives
(optional)

3 tablespoons (60 ml/2 fl oz)
red-wine vinegar

1 teaspoon dried oregano

½ teaspoon dried chilli flakes
(optional)

2 tablespoons chopped fresh
flat-leaf parsley

Heat oil in a small frying pan over low heat. Add the garlic, stir for a few minutes, then add the olives and stir for 1 minute.

Pour in the vinegar, add the oregano, chilli (if using) and parsley, stir and remove from the heat.

Serve olives hot or warm as part of a meze platter with marinated fetta.

Eggplant Dip

Melitzanosalata

1 large eggplant (or 2 medium-sized eggplants)

½ cup (125 ml/4½ fl oz) oil, plus extra for brushing

1 large red capsicum

3 cloves garlic, unpeeled

1 small onion, grated

¾ cup (180 g/6 oz) soft breadcrumbs

100 g (3½ oz) fetta cheese (optional)

juice of 1 lemon

salt and freshly ground black pepper

½ teaspoon ground sweet paprika

2 tablespoons chopped fresh parsley

4 pitted olives, chopped, for garnish

chopped fresh parsley, for garnish

Preheat oven to 180°C (360°F). Line a baking tray with baking paper.

Cut eggplant in half, brush with a little olive oil and place on prepared baking tray along with the capsicum and garlic. Cook in a moderate oven for about 50 minutes, or until soft to the touch. Remove from oven and cool eggplant slightly. Place capsicum in a bowl and cover with cling wrap. When cooled remove skin, deseed and chop flesh.

Peel eggplant, discard skin and chop flesh roughly. Combine eggplant and capsicum flesh with remaining ingredients and place in a food processor. Blend until smooth. >

Season eggplant mixture with salt, pepper and lemon juice. Place in a bowl and refrigerate for at least 2 hours before serving (mixture will thicken when chilled).

Garnish with olives and parsley and a drizzle of olive oil. Serve with toasted pita bread or celery and carrot sticks.

This dip will keep for 2–3 days in the fridge.

Saganaki

Serves 4

milk (or water), for brushing

plain flour, for dusting

**400 g (14 oz) kefalograviera
cheese, cut into 4 even pieces**

**3 tablespoons (60 ml/2 fl oz)
olive oil**

juice of 1 lemon

Brush cheese with milk (or water) and dust with flour.

Heat oil in a frying pan over medium heat. Place the cheese pieces in the pan and fry gently until golden. Then turn to cook the other side.

Remove from pan, place on a serving plater and drizzle with oil from the frying pan and add a squeeze of lemon juice. Serve hot.

Sausages

Loukanika

Makes about 20

250 g (9 oz) pork mince

250 g (9 oz) lamb mince

1 clove garlic, crushed

1 small onion, grated

½ teaspoon ground cinnamon

½ teaspoon dried oregano

1 teaspoon ground
  cumin seeds

salt and freshly ground
  black pepper

½ cup chopped fresh parsley

100 ml (3½ fl oz) sweet sherry

1 cup soft breadcrumbs

1 egg

olive oil for frying

lemon wedges, to serve

tzatziki (page 37) or tomato
  sauce (page 239), to serve

Place all ingredients in a bowl and mix well. Cover and refrigerate overnight.

Using wet hands, shape mixture into small sausages about 8 cm (3 in) long
and 5 cm (2 in) wide.

Grill or shallow-fry sausages over high heat for about 15 minutes, turning
several times, until golden-brown all over.

Remove sausages from grill or frying pan and serve hot with lemon wedges,
tzatziki or tomato sauce.

Beef mince can be used instead of pork and lamb mince.

Spanakopita

½ cup (125 ml/4 fl oz) olive oil

1 small leek, finely chopped

2 cloves garlic, crushed (optional)

1 kg (2 lb 3 oz) baby spinach leaves

½ bunch fresh dill, chopped

½ cup finely chopped fresh flat-leaf parsley

400 g (14 oz) fetta cheese

4 eggs, lightly beaten

2 tablespoons (40 ml/1½ fl oz) freshly squeezed lemon juice

salt and freshly ground black pepper

1 × 375-g (13-oz) packet filo pastry

250 g (9 oz) butter, melted

Preheat oven to 180°C (360°F). Line a baking tray with baking paper.

Heat oil in a frying pan over medium heat. Sauté leek and garlic until soft. Add spinach and cook until wilted (about 5 minutes). Remove pan from heat and allow spinach to cool. Squeeze excess moisture from spinach, then return to the pan.

In a bowl, combine dill, parsley, fetta, eggs and lemon juice, and season with salt and pepper. Add leek and spinach mixture, and mix well.

On a clean work surface, stack three sheets of filo pastry on top of each other, brushing between each sheet with melted butter. Cut pastry lengthways into three strips. >

Place a tablespoonful of mixture at the end of a pastry strip, then fold filo over mixture, tucking in the sides, and continue to roll, brushing pastry with melted butter as you go, to create a log. Repeat with remaining mixture and filo.

Place spanakopita on the prepared baking tray and brush each with melted butter. Place in the preheated oven and bake for about 30 minutes until golden and crisp. Serve hot or warm.

◫ Homemade pastry can be used instead of purchased filo pastry (page 233).

◫ This recipe can also be made in a spiral shape. Leave filo pastry sheets whole, place filling along the edge closest to you, 1½ cm (⅝ in) from the edge. Fold in the edges, then roll pastry into a log shape, brushing the pastry with melted butter along the edge as you roll. Place log on a lined baking tray and coil it into a spiral. Continue with the remaining filling and pastry, placing each additional log around the spiral on the tray until the tray is filled. Brush the spiral with melted butter, sprinkle with sesame seeds and bake in the preheated oven for 40 minutes.

Taramosalata

Makes about 1½ cups

**6 slices stale white sourdough
bread, crusts removed**

100 g (3½ oz) tarama (see note)

**1 small onion, chopped into
quarters (optional)**

**¾ cup (180 ml/6 fl oz) freshly
squeezed lemon juice**

**2 cups (500 ml/17 fl oz)
olive oil**

Place bread in a bowl, cover with warm water and let soak for 10 minutes.
Squeeze out moisture.

Spoon tarama into a small bowl, cover with warm water and let sit for
5 minutes.

Place onion (if using), tarama, bread and lemon juice in a food processor
and blend until mixture is smooth. Slowly drizzle in the olive oil to create a
creamy texture. If too thick, loosen with a little warm water.

Serve with crusty bread, warmed pita or celery and carrot sticks.

Tarama is the salted roe of carp or cod. It can be purchased from
Greek delis.

Greek Meatballs

Keftedes

Makes about 40

500 g (1 lb 2 oz) lamb mince

1 onion, finely chopped

2 small cloves garlic, crushed

1 × 400-g (14-oz) can chopped
tomatoes

1 bunch mint, finely chopped

½ bunch parsley, chopped

1 tablespoon dried oregano

salt and freshly ground
black pepper

1 cup (250 g/8½ oz)
self-raising flour

plain four, for dusting

vegetable oil for shallow-frying

tomato–chilli chutney (page
237) or tzatziki (page 37),
to serve

Combine all ingredients in a mixing bowl. Using your hands, make sure
mixture is thoroughly combined.

Roll tablespoonfuls of the lamb mixture into balls, flatten each slightly and
dust with plain flour.

Heat vegetable oil in a frying pan over medium heat. Shallow-fry keftedes
in batches until both sides are golden (about 4–5 minutes on each side).
Place keftedes on paper towel to drain.

Serve hot or at room temperature with chilli chutney or tzatziki.

Eggplant Fritters

Melitzanokeftedes

Makes 60

⅓ cup (80 ml/3 fl oz) olive oil

1 tablespoon (20 g/¾ oz) butter

1 small leek, finely chopped

1 clove garlic, crushed

2 tablespoons dried oregano

salt

1.5 kg (3 lb 5 oz) eggplants

1 cup grated kefalotiri

2 eggs, lightly beaten

1 teaspoon baking powder

½ cup fresh flat-leaf parsley, finely chopped

½ cup fresh basil

1 tablespoon (20 ml/¾ fl oz) freshly squeezed lemon juice

1 teaspoon ground cumin (optional)

freshly ground black pepper

1¾ cups soft breadcrumbs, plus extra for coating

vegetable oil for frying

tzatziki (page 37) or tomato–chilli chutney (page 237), to serve

Preheat oven to 180°C (360°F). Line baking tray with baking paper.

Heat olive oil and butter in a frying pan over medium heat. Add leek, garlic and half the oregano, and sauté until leek is soft. Season with salt. Remove pan from heat.

Cut eggplants in half, brush with oil, then sprinkle with salt and remaining oregano. Place on prepared baking tray and bake in preheated oven for about 40 minutes or until eggplants are soft.

Remove eggplants from oven and scoop out flesh. Discard the skins, chop the eggplant flesh into small pieces and add to frying pan with leek mixture. Return pan to medium heat and cook, stirring continuously, until eggplant flesh turns golden.

Place eggplant mixture in a bowl and stir in cheese, eggs, baking powder, parsley, basil, lemon juice, cumin (if using), and season with salt and pepper. Mix in enough breadcrumbs to form a soft, pliable mixture. Cover bowl and chill in the refrigerator for about 1 hour.

Spread extra breadcrumbs in a shallow plate. Shape tablespoonfuls of the eggplant mixture into fritters and gently roll in breadcrumbs to coat.

Heat 5 mm (¼ in) vegetable oil in a heavy-based frying pan over high heat. Add the patties, in batches, and shallow-fry until browned underneath (about 3–5 minutes). Turn over and fry for another 3–5 minutes. Remove fritters with a slotted spoon and drain on paper towel.

Serve immediately with tzatziki or tomato–chilli chutney.

Lamb Filo Cigars with Tzatziki

Makes about 30

2 tablespoons (40 ml/1½ oz)
olive oil

1 red onion, finely chopped

2 cloves garlic, crushed

salt

1 teaspoon dried oregano

500 g (1 lb 2 oz) lamb mince

2 tablespoon cumin seeds,
toasted and crushed

1 teaspoon ground cinnamon

1 teaspoon ground allspice

1 × 400-g (14-oz) can
diced tomatoes

freshly ground black pepper

½ cup roughly chopped
walnuts or pistachio nuts

½ cup sultanas (optional)

½ cup chopped fresh parsley

1 × 375-g (13-oz) packet
filo pastry

3 tablespoons (60 g/2 oz)
butter, melted

1 cup grated parmesan
cheese (optional)

tzatziki (page 37) or tomato–
chilli chutney (page 237),
to serve

Preheat oven to 160°C (320°F). Line a baking tray with baking paper.

Heat oil in a heavy-based saucepan over medium heat. Add onion, garlic,
1 teaspoon salt and the oregano, and sauté for 2 minutes until onion is soft.
Add lamb and cook, stirring, until lamb has browned (about 8 minutes). Stir
in cumin, cinnamon, and allspice. Add tomatoes and season with salt and
pepper. Bring to the boil, then reduce heat to low. Cook until most of the
juice has evaporated (about 15 minutes). >

Add nuts and sultanas (if using) to the mixture. Remove pan from heat and let cool. Add parsley and check seasoning.

On a clean work surface, place three sheets of filo pastry one on top of the other, brushing in between each layer with melted butter, and sprinkle the top with parmesan cheese (if using). Cut filo pastry into thirds lengthways, place a tablespoonful of mixture on the short edge of one strip, closest to you. Roll filo over filling and fold edges over, then roll up into a log, brushing with melted butter as you go. Repeat with the remaining filo and mixture.

Place the rolls on the prepared tray, brush tops with melted butter and sprinkle with paprika. Bake in the oven for about 20–30 minutes or until golden-brown.

Serve with tzatziki or tomato chutney.

Cheese Pastries

Tiropitakia

Makes about 36

250 g (9 oz) fetta cheese, crumbled

250 g (9 oz) ricotta cheese, crumbled

250 g (9 oz) kefalotiri, grated

½ cup chopped fresh parsley

2 eggs

freshly ground black pepper

pinch of ground nutmeg

1 × 375-g (13-oz) packet filo pastry

250 g (9 oz) butter, melted

⅓ cup sesame seeds (optional)

Preheat oven to 170°C (340°F). Line a baking tray with baking paper.

Add all the cheeses together in a bowl and mix well. Add parsley, eggs, pepper and nutmeg.

On a clean work surface, place three layers of pastry on top of each other, with melted butter brushed in between each layer. Brush the top sheet with butter and cut pastry into three strips. Place a teaspoonful of cheese mixture at one end of a pastry strip and fold over one corner to make a triangle, then continue folding pastry strip from side to side in the shape of a triangle until you reach the end. Repeat with remaining mixture and pastry.

Put cheese triangles on prepared tray, brush with melted butter and sprinkle with sesame seeds (if using). Bake in the preheated oven for about 20 minutes or until golden-brown. Serve hot.

Tzatziki

Makes about 2½ cups

2 cups (500 ml/17 fl oz)
  Greek-style yoghurt

1 long Continental cucumber,
  peeled and chopped

2 cloves garlic, crushed

salt and freshly ground
  black pepper

1 tablespoon (20 ml/¾ fl oz)
  olive oil

1 tablespoon (20 ml/¾ fl oz)
  freshly squeezed lemon juice

3 tablespoons finely chopped
  fresh dill

1 teaspoon dried oregano

Combine all ingredients in a mixing bowl. Stir well, cover and refrigerate for at least 1 hour before serving to blend the flavours.

Serve as a dip, or as an accompaniment to dishes such as chicken souvlaki or chickpea patties.

For a smoother texture, grate the cucumber instead of chopping it – make sure to squeeze all the juice from the grated cucumber before combining it with other ingredients.

Marinated Fetta

Serves 4–6

250 g (9 oz) fetta cheese
½ cup (125 ml/4 fl oz) olive oil
1 teaspoon dried oregano
freshly ground black pepper
½ teaspoon dried chilli flakes
1 clove garlic (optional), peeled

Mix all ingredients together.

Store in an airtight jar or container and place in the refrigerator until ready to serve.

Serve as part of a meze platter with dolmades, warmed pita and tzatziki.

Pickled Octopus

Htapothi toursi

Serves 6

1 kg (2 lb 3 oz) octopus, cleaned

2 cloves garlic, crushed

½ cup (125 ml/4 fl oz) olive oil

½ cup (125 ml/4 fl oz) red-wine vinegar

salt and freshly ground black pepper

½ teaspoon dried chilli flakes (optional)

1 teaspoon dried oregano

Wash octopus and place in a saucepan. Cover and simmer for about 45 minutes – do not add any water, the octopus will cook in its own juices and turn pink. Drain and allow to cool. When octopus is cool enough to handle, strip the suckers from the tentacles with your hands.

Cut octopus into bite-sized pieces and place in a large bowl. Add the remaining ingredients and mix thoroughly. Cover and refrigerate for 12 hours before serving.

Remove octopus from the liquid and serve as a meze, with a shot of ouzo.

Soups & Salads

The most popular Greek soups are chicken egg–lemon soup (*avgolemono*), fish soup (*psarosoupa*), bean soup (*fasolada*) and lentil soup (*faki soupa*).

Vegetarian soups are very popular during periods of fasting, such as during lent at Easter.

A salad of some sort will always be on the table at a Greek meal.

In summer this may be an aromatic *horiatiki salata*, which makes use of tomatoes and cucumbers when they are at their best. In winter any number of cabbage salads may be offered, or perhaps a beetroot salad. All are very healthy and nutritious.

< Greek Salad (page 44)

Greek Salad

Horiatiki salata

Serves 4

OLIVE OIL & LEMON DRESSING

⅓ cup (80 ml/3 fl oz) olive oil

3 tablespoons (60 ml/2 fl oz)
freshly squeezed lemon juice

2 teaspoons chopped
fresh parsley

2 teaspoons chopped
fresh oregano

1 clove garlic, thinly sliced
(optional)

3 large ripe tomatoes,
each cut into 6 wedges

1 Continental cucumber,
peeled and roughly chopped

1 small red onion, thinly sliced

1 green capsicum,
thinly sliced

10 kalamata olives

100 g (4 oz) fetta cheese,
crumbled

dried oregano, for garnish

chopped fresh parsley,
for garnish

To make dressing, combine all ingredients in a screw-top jar and shake well.

Combine all ingredients (except dressing) in a salad bowl.

Pour the dressing over the salad and sprinkle with oregano. Toss gently and garnish with parsley.

Serve immediately.

Lettuce Salad

Maroulosalata

Serves 4–6

1 medium cos lettuce,
  finely chopped

8 spring onions, chopped

1 bunch dill, chopped

2 tablespoons chopped
  fresh parsley

salt and freshly ground
  black pepper

⅓ cup (80 ml/3 fl oz) olive oil

juice of 1 lemon

Combine all ingredients in a bowl and gently mix together.

Serve immediately.

Beetroot Salad
with Fetta & Walnuts

Batzaria salata

Serves 4–6

1 kg (2 lb 3 oz) tender young
beetroots, trimmed

salt

1 small red onion, sliced

olive oil, for drizzling

1 tablespoon dried oregano

2 handfuls rocket

120 g (4 oz) fetta cheese,
crumbled

⅓ cup coarsely chopped
walnuts

2 tablespoons (40 ml/1½ fl oz)
red-wine vinegar

2 tablespoons (40 ml/1½ fl oz)
olive oil

freshly ground black pepper

2 tablespoons chopped
fresh parsley

Preheat oven to 180°C (360°F). Line a baking tray with baking paper.

Place beetroots in a saucepan, cover with water, add 1 teaspoon salt and
bring to the boil. Reduce heat and simmer for 20 minutes. Drain, and cool
slightly. Peel skin off beetroot, cut in half and place on the prepared baking tray with the onion slices. Drizzle with olive oil, season with salt and
oregano, mix well and bake in the preheated oven for about 30 minutes.
Allow to cool.

Place rocket on a serving platter, arrange beetroot and onion on top and
sprinkle with fetta and chopped walnuts. Dress the salad with vinegar, oil,
salt and pepper, and garnish with parsley.

Radish, Cabbage & Fennel Salad

Serves 4

1 fennel bulb, thinly sliced

½ bunch radishes, trimmed and thinly sliced

100 g (3½ oz) rocket

¼ cabbage, thinly sliced

4 spring onions, thinly sliced

1 cup chopped fresh parsley

1 cup torn fresh mint leaves

100 g (3½ oz) shaved kefalotiri

DRESSING

2 tablespoons (40 ml/1½ fl oz) freshly squeezed lemon juice

⅓ cup (80 ml/3 fl oz) olive oil

1 teaspoon salt

1 teaspoon freshly ground black pepper

1 teaspoon chopped fresh mint

3 tablespoons (60 ml/2 fl oz) white-wine vinegar

To make the dressing, place all ingredients in a screw-top jar and shake well to combine. Set aside until needed.

Place the fennel, radishes, rocket, cabbage, spring onions and parsley in a large bowl and mix together. Stir in dressing and sprinkle with mint and kefalotiri. Serve immediately.

This salad is a great accompaniment to fish.

Grilled Eggplant & Zucchini with Haloumi & Pistachio Nuts

Serves 6–8

500 g (1 lb 2 oz) thin
  eggplants, halved
  lengthways

500 g (1 lb 2 oz) small
  zucchini, halved lengthways

3 tablespoons (60 ml/2 fl oz)
  olive oil

salt and freshly ground
  black pepper

2 tablespoons dried oregano

1 teaspoon ground paprika

1 × 180-g (6½-oz) packet
  haloumi cheese, cut into
  5-mm (¼-in) slices

100 g (3½ oz) rocket

1 bunch flat-leaf parsley

1 bunch basil

½ cup pistachio nuts

DRESSING

1 teaspoon cumin seeds,
  toasted and crushed

1 tablespoon (20 ml/¾ fl oz)
  Greek honey

1 tablespoon (20 ml/¾ fl oz)
  white-wine vinegar

juice of ½ lemon

2 cloves garlic, finely chopped
  (optional)

⅔ cup (160 ml/5½ fl oz)
  extra-virgin olive oil

salt and freshly ground
  black pepper

To make the dressing, whisk the cumin, honey, vinegar, lemon juice and garlic (if using) in a small bowl. Gradually add the oil, whisking continuously until well combined. Season with salt and pepper. >

Preheat a barbecue grill or grill pan to medium heat. Using a sharp knife score the eggplant flesh diagonally. Brush the cut sides of the eggplant and zucchini with olive oil, season with salt, pepper and oregano, and sprinkle with paprika. Grill eggplant and zucchini for 3 minutes on each side or until lightly charred and tender. Transfer to a serving bowl.

Heat remaining oil in a frying pan and fry haloumi pieces for 1–2 minutes on each side, until golden. Remove from pan and drain on paper towel.

Add rocket, parsley and basil to the zucchini and eggplant. Pour in half the dressing and toss to combine. Drizzle on the remaining dressing and scatter with pistachio nuts and haloumi.

Tomato Salad with Fetta

Serves 4

120 g (4 oz) rocket (or baby spinach)

15 kalamata olives

1 small red onion, thinly sliced

1 × 250-g (9-oz) punnet cherry tomatoes, each cut in half

1 cup fresh breadcrumbs

200 g (7 oz) fetta cheese, cut into 4-cm (1½-in) cubes

1 egg, lightly beaten

juice of ½ lemon

3 tablespoons (60 ml/2 fl oz) olive oil, plus extra for frying

salt and freshly ground black pepper

½ cup chopped fresh basil, for garnish

Arrange rocket, olives, onion and tomatoes on a serving platter.

Place breadcrumbs in a shallow bowl. Dip the fetta into the beaten egg, then toss in the breadcrumbs.

In a small bowl, mix together the lemon juice, olive oil, and salt and pepper to taste. Set aside.

Heat oil in a frying pan over medium heat. Add the crumbed cheese and cook until golden, turning occasionally.

Scatter fetta over the salad, drizzle with dressing and garnish with basil. Serve immediately.

Marinated Calamari with Cannellini Beans

Kalamari salata me fasolia

Serves 4

500 g (1 lb 2 oz) squid, cleaned

salt and freshly ground
  black pepper

1 tablespoon (20 ml/¾ fl oz)
  olive oil

1 teaspoon ground paprika

1 × 400-g (14-oz) can
  cannellini beans, drained

3 spring onions, thinly sliced

100 g (3½ oz) rocket

1 cup chopped fresh
  flat-leaf parsley

1 cup chopped fresh basil

juice of 1 lemon

½ teaspoon dried chilli flakes

Slit each squid open and score the underside lightly in a cross-hatch pattern. Transfer to a bowl. Season squid with salt and pepper, add oil and paprika, stirring to coat the squid well.

Heat a griddle pan, wok or barbecue until very hot. Cook the squid for about 1 minute until nicely coloured, then turn and cook for a further minute.

Mix together remaining ingredients and place on a serving platter. Season with salt and pepper. Cut the squid into diagonal slices and arrange on top of the salad. Serve immediately.

Chicken Egg-lemon Soup

Kotosoupa avgolemono

Serves 6–8

1 × 1-kg (2 lb 3-oz) chicken
2 L (4 pt 4 fl oz) boiling water
1 carrot, chopped into 3 pieces
1 onion, halved
1 stick celery
a few peppercorns

salt
½ cup short-grain rice
2 eggs
3 tablespoons (60 ml/2 fl oz)
    freshly squeezed lemon juice
fresh dill, for garnish (optional)

Place chicken in a large saucepan, add boiling water, carrot, onion, celery and peppercorns. Cover and simmer gently for 2 hours or until chicken is tender. Season with salt during the last hour of cooking. Remove chicken from the stock (reserving stock) and set aside to cool.

Strain stock, then return to the saucepan and bring to the boil over medium heat. Add rice, reduce heat, and simmer for 20 minutes. Remove pan from heat.

Whisk eggs until frothy then gradually whisk in lemon juice. Whisk in 2 cups of the hot soup, then whisk egg and lemon mixture into remaining soup. Continue to whisk soup over low heat until it is heated through (do not boil). Check seasoning. Once chicken has cooled, shred flesh, add to soup and serve garnished with dill (if using).

⌑ This soup is best made just before serving.

Fisherman's Soup

Kakavia

Serves 6–8

300 g (10½ oz) medium-sized raw (green) prawns, shelled and deveined (reserve shells)

1 large onion, chopped

2 sticks celery, chopped

1 medium carrot, chopped

2 bay leaves

⅓ cup (80 ml/3 fl oz) olive oil

1 large leek, sliced

3 cloves garlic, thinly sliced

1 × 400-g (14-oz) can chopped tomatoes

grated zest of ½ lemon

½ cup (125 ml/4 fl oz) dry white wine

½ cup medium-grain rice

1 large potato, chopped

1 teaspoon sugar

salt and freshly ground black pepper

250 g (9 oz) firm white fish fillets, cut into 4-cm (1½-in) pieces

150 g (5 oz) scallops

2 tablespoons chopped fresh parsley

1 teaspoon chopped fresh dill (optional)

3 tablespoons (60 ml/2 fl oz) freshly squeezed lemon juice

Combine reserved prawn shells with the onion, half the celery, the carrot, bay leaves and 2 L (4 pt 4 fl oz) water in a large saucepan. Simmer, uncovered, for 35 minutes.

Strain stock, discarding vegetables and prawn shells. Make sure you have 1½ litres (3 pt 3 fl oz) of stock (add a little boiling water if necessary).

Heat oil in a large saucepan over medium heat. Add leek and garlic and sauté until leek is soft. Add remaining celery, the tomatoes, lemon zest and wine. Add rice and boil, uncovered, until vegetables and rice are soft (about 15 minutes).

Stir in stock and simmer, uncovered, for 10 minutes. Add potato, simmer for about 5 minutes or until potato is just tender, then add sugar, salt and ground black pepper.

Add fish to the soup and simmer for 1 minute. Add prawns and simmer for a further minute before adding scallops. Bring soup to the boil, and stir in parsley, dill (if using) and lemon juice.

Serve immediately with crusty bread.

Bean Soup

Fasolada

Serves 6

500 g (1 lb 2 oz) dried haricot beans, soaked in cold water overnight, or 1 × 400-g (14-oz) can

½ cup (125 ml/4 fl oz) olive oil

1 large onion, roughly chopped

2 cloves garlic, crushed

salt

3 ripe tomatoes, roughly chopped

2 tablespoons tomato paste

3 carrots, sliced

3 sticks celery, sliced

1 L (34 fl oz) boiling water

freshly ground black pepper

chopped fresh flat-leaf parsley, for garnish

Drain and rinse beans, then drain again. If using dried beans, place in a large pot and cover with cold water. Bring to the boil, cover, and simmer for around 30 minutes, until almost tender. Drain and set aside.

Heat oil in a heavy-based saucepan over low heat. Add onion, garlic, 1 teaspoon salt and sauté, stirring occasionally, for about 5 minutes. Stir in tomatoes, tomato paste, carrots, celery and boiling water. Bring to the boil, add the drained beans, then reduce heat, cover and simmer for 1½–2 hours (adding more hot water if necessary) until beans are tender. Season to taste.

Serve hot, garnished with parsley.

Fish Soup with Egg & Lemon Sauce

Psarosoupa me avgolemono

Serves 6–8

1.5 kg (3 lb 5 oz) firm white fish fillets, cut into large pieces

salt

juice of 1 lemon, plus extra to serve

1 medium-sized onion, quartered

1 medium-sized carrot, sliced

2 sticks celery with leaves

3 tomatoes, chopped

½ cup (125 ml/4 fl oz) olive oil, plus extra to serve

5 peppercorns

½ cup short-grain rice

1 quantity egg and lemon sauce (page 243)

chopped fresh parsley, for garnish

freshly ground black pepper

mayonnaise (page 238), to serve

Season fish pieces with 1 teaspoon salt and lemon juice. Set aside.

To a large pot add 2 L (4 pt 4 fl oz) water, onion, carrot, celery and tomatoes, 1 teaspoon salt, the oil and peppercorns. Cook over medium heat for 35 minutes. Reduce to a simmer, add the fish and cook slowly for 15–20 minutes.

Remove fish from the pot with a slotted spoon and keep it hot. Strain the stock and cut vegetables into small pieces. Return vegetables and stock to pot, add the rice and cook for further 20 minutes on moderate heat, until rice is cooked. Remove pot from heat.

Make the egg and lemon sauce, then gradually add it to the soup, stirring continuously over low heat. (Make sure soup does not boil or it will curdle.)

Serve soup hot, garnished with parsley and ground pepper.

Place fish on a serving plate and dress with mayonnaise, or olive oil, lemon juice and chopped parsley.

🔲 This dish can be served with steamed green vegetables.

Lentil Soup

Faki soupa

500 g (1 lb 2 oz) green lentils,
rinsed

2 tablespoons (40 ml/1½ fl oz)
olive oil

1 medium onion, chopped

2 cloves garlic, sliced

800 g (1 lb 12 oz) canned
chopped tomatoes

1 large carrot, chopped
(optional)

1 stick celery, chopped
(optional)

1 potato, peeled and chopped
(optional)

½ teaspoon sugar

1 L (34 fl oz) water or chicken
stock

salt and freshly ground
black pepper

2 bay leaves

2 tablespoons (40 ml/1½ fl oz)
white-wine vinegar

1 teaspoon dried oregano

Place lentils in a saucepan, cover with cold water and bring to the boil.
Cook for 5 minutes, then drain, discarding the cooking liquid. (This pre-
vents the lentils from darkening during further cooking.)

Heat oil in a large saucepan over medium heat, add onion and garlic, and
sauté until softened. Stir in lentils and add tomatoes, vegetables (if using)
and sugar. Add water or stock, season with salt and pepper, and bring to
the boil.

Reduce heat, cover and simmer for about 30 minutes. Add bay leaves, vinegar and oregano, and simmer for a further 15 minutes, or until lentils are soft.

Remove bay leaves, sprinkle soup with freshly ground pepper and oregano, and extra oil and vinegar if desired.

Serve immediately.

Vegetables

Many Greek recipes are based on vegetables, and there's a wealth of dishes suitable for vegetarians. The Mediterranean diet is full of richly coloured, healthy vegetables like eggplants, zucchini, capsicums and tomatoes. These may be stuffed with rice or cheese, fried or baked.

Favourite meat dishes such as moussaka can easily become suitable for vegetarians, while baked potatoes are a terrific accompaniment to roasts and skewered meat.

< Stuffed Tomatoes (page 68)

Stuffed Tomatoes

Yemista

Serves 4

8 medium-sized firm
  ripe tomatoes

1 teaspoon sugar

salt

4 small red capsicums

4 medium-sized potatoes,
  peeled and cut into wedges

¾ cup (180 ml/6 fl oz) olive oil

2 tablespoons (40 g/1½ oz)
  butter

1 large onion, finely chopped

1 small leek, finely chopped

2 cloves garlic, thinly sliced

500 g (1 lb 2 oz) beef mince

1 × 400-g (14-oz) can
  chopped tomatoes

½ cup long-grain rice

½ large bunch mint or
  basil, chopped

½ bunch parsley, chopped

freshly ground black pepper

1 cup (250 ml/8½ fl oz)
  tomato purée

juice of ½ lemon

Preheat oven to 200°C (390°F). Grease a large baking dish.

Cut tops off tomatoes and set aside, scoop out tomato flesh, chop and reserve. Sprinkle the insides of the tomatoes with sugar and salt. Cut tops off capsicums and deseed, keeping them intact.

Parboil potatoes in salted water until just soft (about 10 minutes). Drain.

Heat 3 tablespoons of oil and the butter in a heavy-based saucepan over medium heat. Add onion, leek and garlic, and cook for about 10 minutes, until caramelised. Add beef and cook, stirring, until it browns (about 15 minutes). Add canned tomatoes plus reserved tomato flesh. Cook, stirring, for about 5 minutes. Stir in rice, reduce heat and simmer for 8 minutes, stirring continuously.

Remove pan from heat, add herbs and season with salt and pepper. Set aside to cool.

Fill tomato and capsicum cases with rice mixture, then cover tomatoes with the tomato tops. Place in the prepared baking dish. Arrange potato slices between the stuffed vegetables. Drizzle with remaining olive oil, tomato purée and lemon juice. Season with salt and pepper.

Cover baking dish with aluminium foil. Place in preheated oven and bake for 45 minutes. Remove dish from oven, take off foil, baste stuffed vegetables with pan juices and return to oven. Bake, uncovered, for a further 30 minutes until golden-brown.

Serve hot or cold.

Spinach with Rice

Spanakorizo

Serves 4–6

500 g (1 lb 2 oz) baby spinach
 leaves

½ cup (125 ml/4 fl oz) olive oil

1 small leek, finely chopped

2 cloves garlic, thinly sliced

1½ cups medium-grain rice

3½ cups (875 ml/30 fl oz)
 chicken (or vegetable) stock

2 tablespoons finely chopped
 fresh dill (optional)

2 tablespoons finely chopped
 fresh parsley

salt and freshly ground
 black pepper

2 tablespoons (40 ml/1½ fl oz)
 freshly squeezed lemon juice

Heat oil in a saucepan over medium heat. Add leek and garlic, and sauté until leek is soft. Add rice, stirring to coat with the oil. Add 3 cups of the chicken stock, 1 cup (250 ml/8½ fl oz) at a time, waiting for stock to be absorbed before adding next cup. Reduce heat, cover and simmer for 8 minutes, stirring once to make sure rice doesn't stick to bottom of the pan. Stir in spinach and remaining stock, and simmer for a further 3 minutes or until rice is just cooked.

Remove pan from heat and stir in dill (if using) and parsley. Season with salt and pepper and add lemon juice. Serve hot or cold.

Tomato Pilafi

2 tablespoons (40 g/1½ oz) butter

2 tablespoons (40 ml/1½ fl oz) olive oil

1 leek, thinly sliced

2 cloves garlic, crushed

1 red capsicum, chopped

2 cups short-grain rice

1 L (34 fl oz) chicken (or vegetable) stock

1 cup chopped tomatoes

½ cup chopped fresh basil

½ cup chopped fresh parsley

2 tablespoons (40 ml/1½ fl oz) freshly squeezed lemon juice

salt and freshly ground black pepper

Heat butter and oil in a frying pan over medium heat, add leek and garlic, and sauté until soft. Add capsicum and cook until soft. Add rice and cook for about 4 minutes, stirring continuously. Gradually add stock and tomatoes, and stir until beginning to boil.

Reduce heat to low, cover and cook for about 12–15 minutes. Stir in basil, parsley and lemon juice, and season with salt and pepper.

Let stand for about 10 minutes before serving. Serve as a side dish with lamb or chicken.

Potato Mash with Garlic

Skordalia

Serves 6

6–8 cloves garlic, unpeeled

salt

1 cup mashed potato

2 slices stale white bread, crusts removed

⅓ cup (80 ml/3 fl oz) olive oil, plus extra for drizzling

juice of ½ lemon

1 tablespoon (20 ml/¾ fl oz) white-wine vinegar

freshly ground black pepper

Preheat oven to 180°C (360°F). Line a baking tray with baking paper.

Place garlic cloves on prepared baking tray and drizzle with a little olive oil. Place in preheated oven and roast for 20 minutes, until soft. Remove garlic from oven and when slightly cool, peel and crush flesh in a mortar and pestle with a pinch of salt. Add mashed potato and continue to pound.

Soak bread in cold water for 5 minutes or until soft, then squeeze dry. Place potato–garlic mix in a food processor with bread and blend to a smooth paste. Add oil, lemon juice and vinegar, and salt and pepper to taste. Continue to blend until sauce is smooth.

Serve with boiled or fried fish, beetroot salad or fried vegetables.

🔲 Crush garlic with ½ cup roasted almonds or walnuts for variation. Fresh garlic can be used instead of roasted garlic, but will have a much stronger flavour, so only use 3 cloves.

Vegetarian Moussaka

Serves 6

1.5 kg (3 lb 5 oz) potatoes,
  sliced

1 kg (2 lb 3 oz) eggplant,
  sliced thickly

½ cup (125 ml/4 fl oz) olive oil

salt

1 tablespoon dried oregano

1 medium-sized onion,
  finely chopped

2 cloves garlic, sliced

1 medium-sized red capsicum,
  chopped

1 medium-sized green
  capsicum, chopped

800 g (1 lb 12 oz) canned
  chopped tomatoes

½ cup (125 ml/4 fl oz)
  tomato purée

1 teaspoon ground allspice

1 cup chopped fresh parsley

½ teaspoon sugar

freshly ground black pepper

1 tablespoon ground nutmeg

1 cup grated kefalotiri

1 quantity béchamel sauce
  (page 247)

Preheat oven to 180°C (360°F). Grease a 33-cm × 23-cm (13-in × 9-in) baking dish. Line two baking trays with baking paper.

Parboil the potato slices in salted water for 10 minutes. Drain.

Spread potato and eggplant slices on the prepared baking trays. Drizzle with half the oil, and sprinkle with salt and oregano. Bake in the oven for about 30 minutes, turning once. >

Heat remaining oil in a heavy-based saucepan over medium heat. Add onion and garlic, and sauté until soft. Add the capsicums and cook for a further 5 minutes. Add the tomatoes, tomato purée, allspice, parsley, sugar, and salt and pepper to taste. Reduce heat and simmer for 10 minutes until sauce thickens.

To assemble the moussaka, layer half the potato and eggplant slices in the bottom of a baking dish. Pour half the tomato sauce over, sprinkle with ground nutmeg and scatter with a third of the grated cheese. Add another potato–eggplant layer, pour the remaining tomato sauce over and sprinkle with nutmeg and half the remaining cheese. Pour on the béchamel sauce, sprinkle with nutmeg and finish with remaining cheese. Bake in the oven for 50 minutes or until top is golden-brown.

Serve hot or cold with Greek salad.

Greek Baked Beans

Gigantes plaki

Serves 4

1 small eggplant, diced

2 tablespoons (40 ml/1½ fl oz) olive oil, plus extra to serve

1 quantity tomato sauce (page 239)

1 stick celery, chopped

1 carrot, thinly sliced

1 red capsicum, thinly sliced

1 teaspoon cumin seeds, toasted

1 × 400-g (14-oz) can butter beans, drained

juice of ½ lemon

½ cup chopped fresh parsley

½ cup chopped fresh basil

100 g (3½ oz) fetta cheese, crumbled (optional)

Preheat oven to 180°C (360°F).

Lightly fry the eggplant in the olive oil until golden.

Make the tomato sauce as directed, adding the celery, carrots, capsicum, eggplant and cumin to the pan while sautéing the onion.

Place beans in a baking dish, cover with tomato sauce and bake in the preheated oven for 30–40 minutes.

Serve beans warm or cold, drizzled with olive oil and lemon juice, and scattered with parsley, basil and fetta (if using).

Baked Potatoes

Patates sto fourno

Serves 4–6

**1 kg (2 lb 3 oz) potatoes,
peeled and cut into large
wedges**

½ cup (125 ml/4 fl oz) olive oil

juice of 1 lemon

**salt and freshly ground
black pepper**

1 tablespoon dried oregano

Preheat oven to 180°C (360°F). Grease a large baking tray.

Cook potatoes in a large saucepan of salted boiling water for about 10 minutes or until just tender.

Drain potatoes and spread on the prepared baking tray. Score the top of each potato wedge with a fork.

Drizzle oil over the potatoes, add lemon juice and season with salt, pepper and oregano. Bake in the oven for about 40 minutes or until potatoes are crunchy and golden-brown.

Pumpkin Pie

3 cups diced pumpkin

½ cup short-grain rice

3 tablespoons (60 ml/2 fl oz) olive oil

1 large red onion

salt

2 tablespoons (40 g/1½ oz) soft brown sugar

1 cup sultanas

1 teaspoon ground cinnamon

¼ teaspoon ground cloves

freshly ground black pepper

250 g (9 oz) soft goat's cheese or ricotta cheese

1 × 375-g (13-oz) packet filo pastry

250 g (9 oz) butter, melted

sesame seeds, for garnish

Boil the pumpkin for about 5 minutes, until just tender. Drain. Boil the rice for 10–12 minutes. Drain.

Heat oil in a large frying pan over medium heat. Sauté the onion and sprinkle with ½ teaspoon salt. Cook for about 5 minutes on medium heat. Add pumpkin and cook gently for another 5 minutes. Add rice, sugar, sultanas, cinnamon and cloves. Season with salt and pepper, mix well then remove from heat. Place mixture in a bowl and let cool. Cover and refrigerate for a couple of hours. Remove from fridge and add goat's cheese.

Preheat oven to 180°C (360°F). Grease a 35-cm (14-in) round baking dish with melted butter or oil.

Place a sheet of filo pastry on a clean surface. Brush with melted butter then place another sheet of filo pastry on top. Put a line of filling along the edge of the pastry closest to you, about 1.5 cm (⅝ in) in from the edge. Roll up the filling into a cylinder-shape tucking the ends in and brushing the pastry with melted butter as you go.

Coil the pastry roll into a spiral in the centre of the baking dish. Repeat with the remaining mixture and pastry sheets, adding the pastry to the outside of existing spiral to make one big spiral. Sprinkle with sesame seeds and bake for 40 minutes or until golden-brown. Serve warm or cold.

Stuffed Vegetables with Rice

Lahanika yemista me rizi

Serves 4

2 large potatoes,
cut into wedges

4 medium-sized tomatoes

4 medium-sized green
capsicums

4 zucchini

2 tablespoons (30 g/1 oz)
caster sugar

salt

3 tablespoons (60 ml/2 fl oz)
olive oil

1 medium-sized onion,
chopped

1 clove garlic, crushed

1 cup medium-grain rice

1 bunch mint (or dill),
chopped

2 tablespoons tomato paste

2 cups (500 ml/17 fl oz)
tomato purée

freshly ground black pepper

3 tablespoons pine nuts

½ cup (125 ml/4 fl oz) olive oil

1 cup (250 ml/8½ fl oz)
chicken (or vegetable) stock

Preheat oven to 170°C (340°F). Grease a large baking dish.

Parboil the potatoes in salted water until barely tender (about 10 minutes).
Drain.

Slice the tops off the tomatoes and reserve. Scoop out the tomato flesh,
leaving a 5 mm (¼ in) border and making sure not to break the skin. Chop
flesh and set aside.

Sprinkle tomatoes with sugar and salt, and place in the prepared baking dish. Cut tops off the capsicums (reserve) and deseed. Place capsicums in the baking tray. Slice zucchini in half lengthways. Scoop the flesh from the zucchini, chop and set aside, and place zucchini shells on the baking tray.

Heat oil a large frying pan over medium heat. Add the onion, garlic and 1 teaspoon salt, and sauté until onion softens. Add the zucchini and tomato flesh and cook for about 5 minutes. Stir in rice, mint (or dill), tomato paste and half the tomato purée. Season with salt and pepper, cover, reduce heat to low and cook for about 8–10 minutes. Stir in pine nuts.

Fill the tomato, capsicum and zucchini shells three-quarters full with the rice mixture. Place tops on the tomatoes and capsicums and place the potato wedges in between the stuffed vegetables. Pour the remaining tomato purée over the vegetables, sprinkle with salt and pepper, drizzle with olive oil and pour in the stock. Bake in the oven for 1½ hours until vegetables soften and potatoes are golden and crisp.

If the tops of the vegetables start to brown too much, cover the dish with aluminium foil.

Baked Vegetables

Briami

Serves 4

300 g (10½ oz) potatoes

2 large zucchini, sliced
on an angle

1 large eggplant, cut into cubes

2 green capsicums,
cut into chunks

1 large red capsicum,
cut into chunks

2 large red onions, thinly sliced

salt and freshly ground
black pepper

½ cup (125 ml/4 fl oz) olive oil

2 cloves garlic, crushed

800 g (1 lb 12 oz) canned
chopped tomatoes

2 tablespoons dried oregano

1 tablespoon toasted cumin
seeds, crushed

1 teaspoon sugar

2 tablespoons chopped
fresh parsley

2 tablespoons chopped
fresh basil

½ cup chopped fresh parsley,
basil, dill, for garnish

juice of ½ lemon

Preheat oven to 180°C (360°F). Lightly oil a baking dish.

Boil the potatoes in salted water for about 8 minutes. Drain, then cut into wedges. Mix all the vegetables together in the prepared dish, season with salt and pepper and drizzle with oil. In a bowl, combine garlic, tomatoes, oregano, cumin, sugar, parsley and basil. Pour mixture over vegetables. Bake for 45–60 minutes, until vegetables are tender. Garnish with chopped herbs and lemon juice. Serve hot, by itself or accompanied with meat or fish.

Tomato, Fetta & Spinach Pies

Makes 24

2 tablespoons (40 ml/1½ fl oz)
  olive oil

6 spring onions,
  finely chopped

500 g (1 lb 2 oz) baby
  spinach leaves

400 g (14 oz) fetta cheese,
  crumbled

400 g (14 oz) ricotta
  cheese, crumbled

8 eggs, lightly beaten

½ cup chopped fresh basil

½ cup chopped fresh
  flat-leaf parsley

salt and freshly ground
  black pepper

12 sheets filo pastry

125 g (4½ oz) butter, melted

⅔ cup grated parmesan cheese

12 cherry tomatoes,
  cut into quarters

24 basil leaves

Preheat oven to 180°C (360°F). Grease two large 12-hole muffin trays.

Heat oil in a frying pan over medium heat. Sauté spring onions until soft, add spinach, cover and cook until it wilts (about 5 minutes). Remove pan from heat and allow spinach to cool. Squeeze excess liquid from spinach.

Place spinach and spring onions, fetta and ricotta cheeses, eggs, basil and parsley in a bowl and mix well, seasoning with salt and pepper. >

Place a sheet of filo on a clean work surface. Brush with melted butter and sprinkle with parmesan cheese, then place another sheet of filo on top. Repeat until all pastry sheets have been used (you will end up with six double sheets of filo pastry).

Cut each double sheet into eight squares. Press each square into a muffin hole. Brush pastry base with melted butter then place another square on top, again brushing with butter. Repeat until both muffin trays are filled.

Divide the spinach and cheese mixture evenly among the filo cases. Place trays in the preheated oven and bake for 30 minutes or until mixture has set and pastry is crisp and golden.

Remove pies from oven, and place a fresh basil leaf and two pieces of tomato on top. Serve warm.

Vlita with Spinach

Serves 4

1 large bunch vlita (or use
  chicory)

3 tablespoons (60 ml/2 fl oz)
  olive oil

2 cloves garlic, finely sliced

6 spring onions, chopped

salt and freshly ground
  black pepper

juice of 1 lemon

400 g (14 oz) baby spinach

Boil the vlita in salted water for 15–20 minutes, until tender. Drain well.

Heat oil in a saucepan over medium heat, add garlic and spring onions, and sauté until the onions are slightly coloured. Add the vlita, season with salt and pepper, and stir until vlita is coated with oil. Cook for a further minute then remove pan from heat. Add lemon juice and spinach. Stir to combine, then check seasoning.

Serve with any meat or fish dish.

Vlita is also known as amaranth.

Seafood

Greece is almost entirely surrounded by the Mediterranean sea. Greeks consume a lot of seafood; from whitebait, snapper and red mullet to squid, octopus and prawns.

There is nothing better than visiting a local port and watching the fishermen landing their catch of the day. This absolutely fresh seafood is bought, taken home and cooked the Greek way – with lots of lemon, oregano, olive oil and parsley.

< Prawns with Okra & Haloumi (page 92)

Prawns with Okra & Haloumi

Serves 4

500 g (1 lb 2 oz) okra

salt

2 tablespoons (40 ml/1½ fl oz) white vinegar

extra-virgin olive oil

1 onion, sliced into 5 mm (¼ in) pieces

3 cloves garlic, finely chopped

2 tablespoons dried oregano

1 × 400-g (14-oz) can chopped tomatoes

½ cup coarsely chopped fresh flat-leaf parsley, plus extra for garnish

freshly ground black pepper

100 g (3½ oz) haloumi cheese, sliced

500 g (1 lb 2 oz) medium-sized raw (green) prawns, shelled and deveined

1 tablespoon (20 ml/¾ fl oz) freshly squeezed lemon juice

Cut tops off okra. Sprinkle with salt and vinegar, and stand in a colander for 10 minutes. Rinse thoroughly and pat dry with paper towel.

Heat about 1 tablespoon of the oil in a saucepan over medium heat. Add onion, garlic, a pinch of salt and the oregano. Fry, stirring, for about 3 minutes.

Add okra to the pan, along with the tomatoes, 1 tablespoon oil, parsley, ½ teaspoon salt and pepper to taste. Reduce heat to low, cover pan and cook until okra is soft (20–30 minutes).

Heat about 1 tablespoon olive oil in a frying pan over medium heat. Add haloumi pieces and fry until golden, about 2–3 minutes on each side. Set aside.

Drizzle prawns with 1 tablespoon oil and season with salt.

Heat frying pan over medium–high heat. Add prawns and sauté until pink and starting to turn crisp and golden-brown (about 2 minutes on each side).

To serve, place okra in a shallow serving bowl, arrange prawns over the top and scatter with grilled haloumi pieces. Finish with a squeeze of lemon juice.

Red Mullet with Anchovies & Olives

Serves 4

⅓ cup (80 ml/3 fl oz) olive oil, plus extra for drizzling

1 leek, thinly sliced

2 cloves garlic, thinly sliced

½ fennel bulb, finely chopped

1 tablespoon dried oregano

1 × 400-g (14-oz) can chopped tomatoes

6 anchovy fillets, chopped

10 pitted kalamata olives, chopped

½ cup (125 ml/4 fl oz) white wine (optional)

2 strips lemon zest

800 g (1 lb 12 oz) red mullet fillets (or use any white fish)

juice of 1 lemon

salt

1 teaspoon chopped fresh dill

Heat oil in a frying pan over medium heat. Add leek, garlic, fennel and oregano, and sauté, stirring, until soft (about 6 minutes). Add tomatoes, anchovies, olives, wine (if using) and lemon zest, and cook for a further 5 minutes, stirring.

Place the fish fillets on top of the tomato sauce, and drizzle with olive oil and half the lemon juice. Cover pan, reduce heat and cook for about 10–15 minutes (the fish will steam cook and take the lovely flavours from the sauce). Once fish is cooked, add a pinch of salt, sprinkle with dill, add the remaining lemon juice and serve immediately.

Baked Snapper with Tomato, Onion & Lemon

Psari plaki

Serves 4

1 × 1.5-kg (3 lb 5-oz) snapper (or other whole fish), cleaned

1 red onion, finely chopped

2 cloves garlic, chopped

salt and freshly ground black pepper

½ cup (125 ml/4 fl oz) olive oil, plus extra for drizzling

1 lemon, sliced

1 cup mixed chopped fresh parsley and basil

1 tablespoon dried oregano

juice of 1 lemon

½ cup pitted kalamata olives

12 cherry tomatoes, halved

Preheat oven to 220°C (430°F).

On a baking tray, place a double thickness of aluminium foil big enough to wrap the fish. Spread onion and garlic in the centre of the foil. Place fish on top, season with salt and pepper (inside and outside) and rub with olive oil. Place lemon slices and half the parsley and basil inside the cavity. Sprinkle oregano and lemon juice over fish and top with tomatoes, olives and a drizzle of olive oil.

Fold the foil up around the fish and seal to make a tight parcel. Place tray in the oven and bake for about 40 minutes or until fish is cooked. Let fish stand at room temperature for about 5 minutes before unwrapping. Serve with steamed vegetables or a crispy salad.

Prawns with Rice & Peas

Serves 6

1 tablespoon (20 ml/¾ fl oz) olive oil

1 medium-sized leek, thinly sliced

3 cloves garlic, crushed

salt

1 teaspoon dried oregano

400 g (14 oz) medium-grain rice

1 cup (250 ml/8½ fl oz) dry white wine

1½ L (3 pt 3 fl oz) chicken stock

400 g (14 oz) raw (green) prawns, shelled and deveined

1 cup fresh peas

1 cup chopped fresh basil

1 cup fresh flat-leaf parsley

juice and grated zest of 1 lemon

90 g (3 oz) butter

freshly ground black pepper

Heat oil in a heavy-based saucepan over low heat, add leek, garlic, 1 teaspoon salt and oregano, and sauté gently until leek is soft (about 4 minutes). Add rice, increase heat to medium, stir, add wine and cook for about 2 minutes. Add 2 cups (500 ml/ 17 fl oz) stock, reduce heat slightly and stir. Continue to add stock, 1 cup at a time, stirring gently and allowing each cup to be absorbed before adding the next. (This should take about 15 minutes.)

Add prawns and peas, and simmer for about 3 minutes. Stir in basil, parsley, lemon juice and zest, and butter. Season with salt and pepper, then cook for a further 2 minutes. Serve immediately.

Barbecued Calamari with Skordalia

Serves 4

500 g (1 lb 2 oz) squid, cleaned

½ cup chopped fresh parsley

3 tablespoons chopped fresh dill

1 cup roughly chopped rocket

1 cup roughly chopped roasted almonds

juice of 1 lemon

1 quantity skordalia (page 73)

MARINADE

3 tablespoons (60 ml/2 fl oz) olive oil

1 tablespoon dried oregano

¼ teaspoon ground paprika

2 cloves garlic, crushed

¼ teaspoon dried chilli flakes (optional)

salt and freshly ground black pepper

To make the marinade, combine oil, oregano, paprika, garlic, chilli (if using), salt and pepper in a bowl. Mix well, and set aside.

Rinse squid and pat dry. Cut into strips, score the underside of each piece and place in the marinade. Leave in the refrigerator for 1 hour.

Heat the barbecue to medium–high. Cook the squid, scored side down, for about 2 minutes then turn over and cook for another minute. (The squid will roll up and look like a cone – do not cook for too long or it will become very tough.)

In a bowl, mix parsley, dill and rocket, then combine with the squid pieces.

Stir almonds into skordalia.

Arrange squid on a serving platter and season with salt, pepper and lemon juice. Serve with the skordalia.

Fried Calamari

Serves 2–4

500 g (1 lb 2 oz) small
  squid, cleaned and cut
  into 1.5-cm (1-in) strips

plain flour, for dusting

corn oil or vegetable oil
  for deep-frying

chopped parsley, for garnish

freshly squeezed lemon juice,
  to serve

salt

BEER BATTER

½ cup (75 g/2½ oz) self-
  raising flour

½ cup (75 g/2½ oz) cornflour

salt and freshly ground
  pepper

1 cup (250 ml/8½ fl oz) beer
  (or soda water)

To make the batter, sift flours with a pinch of salt and pepper into a bowl. Make a well in the centre and pour in the beer (or soda water). Gradually stir liquid into the flour until a smooth, thin batter forms. (Try not to overmix.) Let batter stand at room temperature for about 1 hour.

Score the underside of the squid pieces and dust with flour.

Heat oil to 180°C (360°F) in a pan suitable for deep-frying.

Dip each squid piece into the batter then deep-fry a few at a time until they are golden-brown and rise to surface. Remove with a slotted spoon and place on paper towel to drain. Serve garnished with parsley, lemon juice and salt.

Stuffed Calamari

Kalamari yemista

Serves 4–6

½ cup (125 ml/4 fl oz) olive oil

1 tablespoon (20 g/¾ oz) butter

1 leek, thinly sliced

2 cloves garlic, thinly sliced

½ cup medium-grain rice

100 g (3½ oz) pine nuts

1 cup (250 ml/8½ fl oz) chicken stock

salt and freshly ground black pepper

½ cup chopped fresh parsley

½ cup chopped fresh dill

1 kg (2 lb 3 oz) medium-sized squid, cleaned

1½ cups (375 ml/12½ fl oz) tomato sauce (page 239)

½ cup (125 ml/4 fl oz) white wine

Preheat oven to 180°C (360°F). Grease a large baking dish.

Heat half the oil and the butter in a saucepan over medium heat, add leek and garlic, and sauté until leek is soft. Add rice, pine nuts, chicken stock and salt and pepper. Stir over medium heat for about 10 minutes, until rice has absorbed the stock. Take the pan off the heat and stir in parsley and dill.

Partially fill each squid with the rice mixture, leaving room for the rice to swell. Secure the opening with a steel skewer. Arrange stuffed squid in a baking dish.

Heat tomato sauce in a saucepan over low heat. Add wine, and salt and pepper to taste, and simmer for about 5 minutes.

Pour tomato sauce over the squid, cover dish with aluminium foil and place in the preheated oven. Bake for about 45 minutes, then remove foil and bake for a further 20 minutes or until the squid is tender and the sauce is thickened.

Serve hot or cold.

Octopus, Onion & Wine Stew

Htapothi stifado

Serves 8

2 tablespoons (40 ml/1½ fl oz) olive oil

1 large onion, chopped

salt

1 teaspoon dried oregano

3 cloves garlic, crushed

1 kg (2 lb 3 oz) octopus, cleaned

1 cup (250 ml/8½ fl oz) red wine

3 tablespoons (60 ml/2 fl oz) red-wine vinegar

400 g (14 oz) ripe tomatoes, chopped

1 cup (250 ml/8½ fl oz) tomato purée

2 tablespoons tomato paste

1 cinnamon stick

4 cloves

1 teaspoon sugar

1 tablespoon black peppercorns

2 bay leaves

500 g (1 lb 2 oz) small pickling onions or shallots, peeled

freshly ground black pepper

1 cup chopped fresh parsley

100 g (3½ oz) fetta cheese, crumbled (optional)

Heat oil in a heavy-based saucepan over medium heat, add the onion, 1 teaspoon salt and the oregano. Sauté until onion turns slightly brown (about 5 minutes). Stir in garlic, add octopus and stir so octopus is coated in the onion mixture. Add wine, vinegar, fresh tomatoes, tomato purée and paste, cinnamon, cloves, sugar, peppercorns and bay leaves. >

Bring sauce to the boil, add the whole onions or shallots, reduce heat to low and simmer for 1–1½ hours or until the octopus is very tender and the sauce has thickened. Season with salt and pepper, and add parsley and fetta (if using).

Serve immediately with salad, warm skordalia (page 73), or baked potatoes (page 78).

Octopus in Tomato Sauce

Serves 4

1 kg (2 lb 3 oz) octopus,
  cleaned and washed

1 cup (250 ml/8½ fl oz)
  olive oil

1 small leek, finely sliced

2 cloves garlic, crushed

1 tablespoon dried oregano

800 g (1 lb 12 oz) canned
  chopped tomatoes

1 cup (250 ml/8½ fl oz)
  tomato purée

½ cup (125 ml/4 fl oz)
  white wine

½ cup finely chopped
  fresh parsley

½ teaspoon freshly
  ground black pepper

juice of 1 lemon

1 tablespoon chopped
  fresh parsley

1 cup medium-grain rice

½ cup grated kefalotiri

Preheat oven to 180°C (360°F). Grease a large ovenproof dish.

Place octopus in a saucepan, cover and simmer for 15 minutes (do not add any water). Drain. Cut octopus into small pieces and return to saucepan. Add remaining ingredients (except rice and cheese) and cook over low heat, covered until tender and sauce is thick (about 45 minutes).

Meanwhile, cook the rice in salted boiling water for about 15 minutes or until tender. Drain and transfer to prepared dish. Pour tomato sauce over, sprinkle with kefalotiri and bake for about 10 minutes. Serve immediately.

Baked Prawns with Fetta

Garithes youvetsi

Serves 4

½ cup (125 ml/4 fl oz) olive oil

1 leek, thinly sliced

3 cloves garlic, thinly sliced

800 g (1 lb 12 oz) canned chopped tomatoes

½ cup (125 ml/4 fl oz) white wine

½ bunch parsley, chopped

½ teaspoon dried oregano

½ teaspoon sugar

salt and freshly ground black pepper

16 large raw (green) prawns, shelled and deveined, but tail left on

120 g (4 oz) fetta cheese

finely chopped fresh dill, for garnish

Preheat oven to 200°C (390°F). Grease a large baking dish or four ovenproof ramekins.

Heat oil in a frying pan over medium heat. Add leek and cook until transparent. Add garlic, tomatoes, wine, herbs, sugar, salt and pepper. Cover, reduce heat and simmer gently until sauce has reduced (about 20 minutes).

If using a large dish, spoon half the tomato mixture into the dish, arrange prawns on top, then spoon over remaining sauce. If using ramekins, divide half the tomato mixture between the four prepared dishes. Place four prawns in each dish and spoon remaining tomato mixture over. Crumble fetta over the top. Bake for 20–30 minutes, until prawns are cooked and fetta is soft. Serve immediately, garnished with dill.

Char-grilled Octopus
& Roasted Vegetables

Serves 4

1 kg (2 lb 3 oz) baby octopus, cleaned and large octopus cut in half

1½ red capsicums, cut into 2-cm (¾-in) pieces

2 small eggplants, cut into 2-cm (¾-in) pieces

3 red onions, cut into wedges

3 zucchini, cut into 2-cm (¾-in) slices

½ cup (125 ml/4 fl oz) olive oil

salt and freshly ground black pepper

1 teaspoon dried oregano

1 cup mixed fresh parsley and basil

1½ cups (375 ml/12½ fl oz) tzatziki (page 37)

DRESSING

⅔ cup (160 ml/5½ fl oz) olive oil

2 tablespoons (40 ml/1½ fl oz) freshly squeezed lemon juice

1 clove garlic, crushed

salt and freshly ground black pepper

Preheat oven to 200°C (390°F).

Combine dressing ingredients in a bowl and season with salt and pepper. Set aside.

Place baby octopus in a glass bowl and pour half the dressing over. Cover with cling wrap and refrigerate for about 1 hour. >

Combine capsicum, eggplant, onion and zucchini in a roasting pan. Add oil, salt, pepper and oregano. Mix well. Place pan in the preheated oven and bake for about 30 minutes, or until vegetables are golden and tender (turn vegetable once during cooking). Remove from oven, allow to cool, then toss gently with fresh herbs.

Heat a barbecue to very hot and cook octopus for about 8 minutes on each side. Remove from barbecue and cut octopus, on an angle, into large pieces.

To serve, place vegetable salad on a serving platter, drizzle with tzatziki, then top with octopus and pour over remaining dressing.

Fried Whitebait

Serves 4

½ cup (125 ml/4 fl oz) olive oil

1 onion, thinly sliced

2 cloves garlic, thinly sliced

500 g (1 lb 2 oz) whitebait

plain flour, seasoned with
   salt, pepper and oregano,
   for coating

1 cup chopped fresh
   flat-leaf parsley

juice from 1 lemon

Heat 3 tablespoons of the oil in a frying pan over medium heat. Add onion and garlic and sauté until soft (about 3–4 minutes).

In a bowl mix together fish and cooked onion and garlic.

Coat fish with seasoned flour.

Heat remaining oil in a non-stick frying pan and fry fish in batches for 4–5 minutes, turning often, until golden and crisp. Remove using a slotted spoon and drain on paper towel. Season with salt and pepper.

Serve hot garnished with parsley and a squeeze of lemon juice.

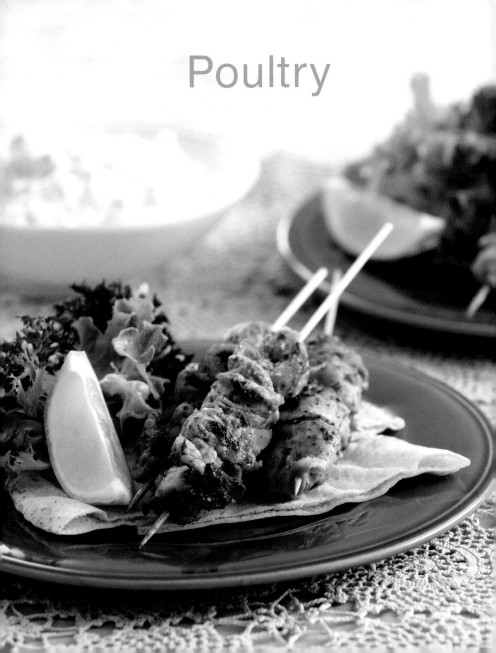

Poultry

In Greece the most popular way to cook poultry is on top of the stove, in a rich, aromatic sauce, and this is usually served with pasta or rice. Poultry may also be roasted for a Sunday dinner, or marinated and barbecued. Chicken is skewered, then flame-cooked for one of the most popular of Greek dishes, souvlaki.

The majority of chickens in Greece are corn fed, which gives their meat a rich, full flavour.

‹ Chicken Souvlaki (page 118)

Chicken Souvlaki

Serves 4

800 g (1 lb 12 oz) skinless
   chicken thigh fillets (or
   use pork or lamb), cut into
   2.5-cm (1-in) cubes

2 tablespoons dried oregano

2 tablespoons dried rosemary

⅓ cup (80 ml/3 fl oz) olive oil

3 tablespoons (60 ml/2 fl oz)
   freshly squeezed lemon juice

grated zest of ½ lemon
   (optional)

1 clove garlic, crushed

salt and freshly ground
   black pepper

1 teaspoon ground paprika
   (optional)

1 teaspoon dried chilli flakes
   (optional)

8 bamboo skewers, soaked
   in water for 30 minutes

lemon wedges, to serve

pita bread, to serve

tzatziki (page 37), to serve

In a large bowl, combine chicken pieces with all other ingredients. Mix well, cover with cling wrap and refrigerate for about 1 hour.

Thread chicken pieces onto prepared bamboo skewers and reserve the remaining marinade.

Heat barbecue (or heavy-based frying pan) to medium heat. Cook skewers for about 10 minutes, basting chicken frequently with marinade, and turning often to cook chicken evenly. Serve skewers immediately with lemon wedges, pita bread, tzatziki and a salad.

Barbecued Poussin

Kotopoulo sta karvouna

Serves 4

2 × 500-g (1 lb 2-oz) poussins,
  cut into quarters

MARINADE

1 cup (250 ml/8½ fl oz) olive oil

juice and grated zest of
  1 orange (optional)

2 cloves garlic, crushed

2 tablespoons honey

3 tablespoons (60 ml/2 fl oz)
  dry white wine

1 tablespoon dried oregano

1 tablespoon chopped fresh
  thyme

1 tablespoon fresh rosemary

1 tablespoon toasted cumin
  seeds, crushed

Combine marinade ingredients in a bowl. Mix well and brush over the chicken pieces. Place chicken on a plate, cover with cling wrap and refrigerate for about 2 hours, brushing with the marinade every 30 minutes. Drain chicken pieces and reserve the marinade.

Heat barbecue to medium. Cook the chicken pieces, turning and basting until they are golden (about 20–30 minutes).

Serve immediately with baked potatoes (page 78), Greek salad (page 44), tzatziki (page 37) and grilled pita bread.

Chicken Pie

Kotopita

Serves 6

3 tablespoons (60 g/2 oz)
butter

3 tablespoons (60 ml/2 fl oz)
olive oil

1 leek, thinly sliced

2 cloves garlic, crushed

1 kg (2 lb 3 oz) chicken thigh
fillets, cut into 2.5-cm (1-in)
pieces

1 tablespoon dried oregano

salt

1½ tablespoons (20 g/¾ oz)
plain flour

¾ cup (180 ml/6 fl oz) white
wine

1 cup (250 ml/8½ fl oz)
chicken stock

1 cup (250 ml/8½ fl oz) milk

freshly ground black pepper

2 eggs, lightly beaten

1 cup grated kefalotiri

1 cup chopped fresh
flat-leaf parsley

1 cup chopped fresh basil

1 tablespoon Dijon mustard

500 g (1 lb 2 oz) spinach

10 sheets filo pastry

200 g (7 oz) butter, melted

sesame seeds, for garnish
(optional)

Preheat oven to 180°C (360°F). Lightly grease a 23-cm (9-in) round pie dish
and line with baking paper.

Heat butter and oil in a large heavy-based saucepan over medium heat.
Add leek and garlic, and sauté until soft. Add chicken, oregano and 1 teaspoon salt, and stir. Cook for about 15 minutes, stirring occasionally. >

Increase heat, add flour, stir for 2 minutes then add wine, chicken stock and milk. Season with salt and pepper. Reduce heat, cover and simmer for 20 minutes, stirring occasionally, until the chicken is tender. Remove saucepan from heat and stir in eggs, cheese, herbs, mustard and spinach.

Layer five sheets of pastry in the pie dish, to line it, brushing with melted butter between each sheet. Pour filling into lined dish, fold over any filo corners and then cover filling with another five sheets of pastry, again brushing with melted butter between each sheet. Tuck in pastry around the edges, brush top of pie with extra melted butter, then score the top into serving-size pieces and sprinkle with sesame seeds (if using). Bake in the preheated oven for 35–40 minutes or until golden-brown. Serve hot.

Chicken with Pilafi

Serves 4

**1 × 1.3-kg (2 lb 14-oz) chicken,
  cut into 4 portions**

salt

125 g (4½ oz) butter

2 cups medium-grain rice

freshly ground black pepper

freshly squeezed lemon juice (optional)

Place chicken in a large saucepan, cover with water, add 1 teaspoon salt and bring to the boil. Reduce heat and simmer for about 1 hour. Remove chicken from pot and save 1 L (34 fl oz) of the stock. Keep chicken pieces warm.

Heat butter in a saucepan over medium heat. Add rice and fry until golden-brown. Stir in stock and season. Cover, reduce heat and simmer for 18–20 minutes or until liquid is absorbed and rice is tender. Remove from heat and leave to stand for 10 minutes. Use a fork to fluff up rice and add lemon juice (if using). Serve with the chicken.

An alternate way of cooking pilafi is to wash and drain rice well, then in a saucepan with a tight lid, bring stock to boil and add rice. Cook, covered, over low heat for 15 minutes or until all liquid is absorbed. Add ½ cup melted butter, then use a fork to fluff up the rice.

Chicken Stew with Tomato Sauce & Square Noodles

Kotopoulo kokkinisto me hilopites

Serves 4

400 g (14 oz) square noodles (*hilopites*) or risoni pasta

3 tablespoons (60 ml/2 fl oz) olive oil

1 × 1-kg (2 lb 3-oz) chicken, cut into 8 pieces

1 large onion, finely chopped

2 cloves garlic, thinly sliced

salt

1 teaspoon dried oregano

800 g (1 lb 12 oz) canned chopped tomatoes

2 cups (500 ml/17 fl oz) tomato purée

½ cup (125 ml/4½ fl oz) white wine

1 teaspoon sugar

1 cinnamon stick

½ teaspoon ground cinnamon

½ teaspoon ground allspice

freshly ground black pepper

2 cups (500 ml/17 fl oz) chicken stock

½ cup grated kefalotiri

1 cup chopped fresh parsley

Cook square noodles (or risoni) in salted boiling water until just tender. Drain.

Heat the oil in a large frying pan over medium heat. Add chicken pieces and cook, turning frequently, for about 8 minutes or until lightly browned all over. Remove with a slotted spoon and set aside. Add the onion and garlic to the pan, along with 1 teaspoon salt and the oregano. Cook over low heat, stirring occasionally, for 5 minutes or until soft. >

Return chicken to the pan, pour in the chopped and puréed tomatoes, add wine, sugar and spices, and season to taste with salt and pepper. Cover and simmer for about 30 minutes.

Stir in the pasta and add half the chicken stock, and simmer for 10 minutes, stirring so the noodles don't stick to the bottom of the saucepan. (If the sauce becomes too dry, add remaining stock, stir and simmer for a further 10 minutes.) Remove stew from heat, and stir in cheese and chopped parsley. Serve hot.

Chicken thigh fillets cut into large pieces can be used instead of a whole chicken.

Roast Chicken with Nut Stuffing

Serves 4

½ cup chopped fresh parsley and basil

1 tablespoon (20 g/¾ oz) softened butter

salt and freshly ground black pepper

1 × 1.3-kg (2 lb 4-oz) chicken

1 cup bread and pistachio stuffing (page 246) or rice, sultana and pine nut stuffing (page 244)

½ orange

½ cup (125 ml/4 fl oz) olive oil, plus extra for rubbing

½ teaspoon ground paprika

1 teaspoon dried oregano

½ cup (125 ml/4 fl oz) chicken stock

Preheat oven to 220°C (430°F).

In a bowl, mix together the herbs, butter, salt and pepper.

Rub chicken cavity with salt, then separate the skin of the breast from the meat with your finger, making two tunnels, one over each breast. Push half the herb butter into each tunnel. Place the stuffing into the large cavity of the chicken, then insert the orange half to keep the stuffing in place. >

Tie the legs together with string as tightly as you can. With your hands rub a little olive oil into the skin of the chicken and season with salt, pepper and paprika (this will give the chicken a nice colour) and sprinkle with dried oregano.

Pour olive oil into the bottom of a baking dish, then put in the chicken, breast-side down. Place in the preheated oven and cook for about 15 minutes. Remove from oven, turn the chicken over and baste it with juices from the pan. Add stock and return to the oven for about 1 hour or until chicken is cooked. (Test by inserting a fork or skewer into the thigh – if juices run out it needs a further 10 minutes.)

Serve with your favourite salad or pilafi.

You can substitute 2 sprigs rosemary, 2 cloves garlic and 1 lemon (cut in half) for the stuffing.

Oven-roasted Poussin Stuffed with Fetta & Basil

Serves 4

400 g (14 oz) chat potatoes

4 × 500-g poussins, cut in half

2½ tablespoons (50 ml/1¾ fl oz)
olive oil, plus extra for
basting

2 tablespoons dried oregano

salt and freshly ground
black pepper

1 red onion, thinly sliced

6 cloves garlic

1 red capsicum, chopped

500 g (1 lb 2 oz) cherry
tomatoes

15 pitted kalamata olives

6 sprigs rosemary

2 tablespoons (40 ml/1½ fl oz)
freshly squeezed lemon juice

1 tablespoon (20 g/¾ fl oz)
butter

STUFFING

300 g (10½ oz) fetta cheese

1½ tablespoons kefalograviera
cheese

2 tablespoons finely chopped
fresh basil

1 clove garlic, crushed

salt and freshly ground
black pepper

Preheat oven to 220°C (430°F). Lightly grease a baking dish.

Parboil the potatoes in salted water for about 10 minutes. Drain.

Combine all the stuffing ingredients in a bowl and season with salt
and pepper. >

Gently slide your fingers under the skin of poussins to create a pocket, and spoon in the stuffing. Rub each piece of chicken with oil, oregano, salt and pepper.

Place poussins in prepared baking dish, skin side down, and add onion, garlic, capsicum, tomatoes, olives, rosemary and oil. Season with salt and pepper.

Cook in preheated oven for about 30 minutes. Remove baking dish from oven, turn poussins over and add potatoes and butter. Spoon juices from pan over the potatoes then return dish to oven. Cook for about 30 minutes, until potatoes are golden. (Increase oven temperature for the last 10 minutes if needed.)

Remove poussins from oven and let stand for about 10 minutes before serving.

Grilled Quail

Ortikia tiganita

Serves 4

8 quail, cut in half
½ cup (125 ml/4 fl oz) olive oil
salt and freshly ground
   black pepper
2 tablespoons dried oregano
1 tablespoon ground paprika

juice and grated zest
   of 1 lemon
2 cloves garlic, crushed
chopped fresh parsley,
   for garnish
chopped fresh basil,
   for garnish

Rub each quail piece with oil, salt and pepper, oregano, paprika, lemon zest and garlic. Cover and refrigerate for about 1 hour.

Preheat barbecue to high. Reduce heat to medium then place quail, wing side down on the barbecue and cook for about 6 minutes, then turn and cook for about 6 minutes more.

Serve immediately, garnished with fresh herbs and a squeeze of lemon juice.

🔳 This dish is perfect as an entrée.

Meat

Meats such as lamb, beef and pork have traditionally been quite uncommon in Greek cuisine due to cost and a lack of availability. Nowadays they have become more plentiful due to an increase in imported produce. This has given rise to the installation of wood-fired ovens in many houses, so that Greeks can enjoy the pleasure of old-fashioned village-style cooking.

For the most part, meat dishes are cooked with plenty of aromatic herbs and spices, and are accompanied by pasta or rice. The most common meats used in Greece are lamb and pork.

< Lamb Baked with Risoni (page 136)

Lamb Baked with Risoni

Youvetsi me kritharaki

Serves 5

3 tablespoons (60 g/2 oz) butter

3 tablespoons (60 ml/2 fl oz) olive oil

1.5 kg (3 lb 5 oz) leg of lamb, diced

1 large onion, chopped

3 cloves garlic, crushed

salt

1 tablespoon dried oregano

3 cups (750 ml/25 fl oz) tomato purée

800 g (1 lb 12 oz) canned chopped tomatoes

2 tablespoons tomato paste

½ teaspoon sugar

freshly ground black pepper

1 cinnamon stick

1 teaspoon ground allspice

2 cups (500 ml/17 fl oz) chicken stock

500 g (1 lb 2 oz) risoni

1 cup grated kefalotiri

Preheat oven to 180°C (360°F). Grease a baking dish with butter.

Heat butter and oil in a heavy-based saucepan over medium heat. Add meat and cook until browned on all sides (about 15 minutes), then remove from pan and set aside.

Add onion, garlic, salt and oregano to the pan and sauté until soft. Add puréed and chopped tomatoes, tomato paste, sugar, pepper, cinnamon and allspice. Stir and return meat to pan.

Pour in stock and bring to the boil, making sure meat is covered with liquid (add more stock if necessary). Reduce heat and simmer, covered, until meat is tender (about 1 hour), adding more stock if necessary.

Boil risoni in salted water until just tender. Drain. Transfer half the risoni to the prepared baking dish. Cover the pasta with half the meat sauce, then sprinkle with half the cheese. Add remaining risoni, pour remaining meat sauce on top and sprinkle with remaining cheese.

Cover dish with aluminium foil and bake in the preheated oven for about 45 minutes or until top is golden and cheese had melted. Remove dish from oven and let it sit for 5 minutes before serving.

Pastitsio

500 g (1 lb 2 oz) tubular
  spaghetti

½ cup (125 ml/4 fl oz) olive oil

1 large onion, finely chopped

2 cloves garlic, crushed

salt

1 teaspoon dried oregano

500 g (1 lb 2 oz) lamb mince

500 g (1 lb 2 oz) pork mince

800 g (1 lb 12 oz) canned
  chopped tomatoes

2 tablespoons tomato paste

1 cinnamon stick

1 teaspoon ground cinnamon

½ teaspoon mixed spice

½ teaspoon sugar

½ cup chopped fresh parsley

½ cup (125 ml/4 fl oz) red wine

freshly ground black pepper

1 egg, separated and white
  lightly beaten

2 cups grated kefalograviera
  cheese

1 L (34 fl oz) béchamel sauce
  (page 247)

Preheat oven to 180°C (360°F). Grease a 24-cm × 28-cm (9½-in × 11-in)
baking dish with oil.

Cook spaghetti in salted boiling water until al dente (about 14 minutes).
Strain and allow to cool.

Heat olive oil in a large heavy-based saucepan over low–medium heat. Add
onion, garlic, 1 teaspoon salt and the oregano, and sauté, stirring, for about
5 minutes until soft. >

Add mince and cook, stirring, until meat browns. Stir in the tomatoes, tomato paste, cinnamon stick, mixed spice, sugar, parsley and wine, and season with salt and pepper. Reduce heat and simmer for about 50 minutes, or until the sauce has thickened. Fold the egg white and ½ cup kefalograviera into the sauce.

Add 1 cup béchamel sauce and 1 cup kefalograviera to the cooled pasta. Spread half the pasta over the base of the prepared baking dish. Spread half the meat mixture on top, then sprinkle with a third of the remaining cheese and a third of the ground cinnamon. Cover meat layer with remaining pasta, then pour over remaining meat sauce. Sprinkle with half the remaining cheese and ground cinnamon. Pour remaining béchamel sauce over the meat sauce and sprinkle with the remaining cheese and ground cinnamon.

Bake for 50 minutes until golden-brown. Let pastitsio stand in the dish for 15 minutes before serving. Serve hot with a salad.

▣ You can substitute filo pastry for the béchamel sauce. Place eight layers of filo on the bottom of the baking dish (brush between sheets with melted butter), then follow recipe as above. When last layer of meat is poured into dish and covered with cheese and cinnamon, place another eight sheets of filo pastry on top (brushed between with melted butter) and brush top with melted butter. Score the top layers of pastry into serving-sized pieces and bake for 40–50 minutes or until pastry is golden. Turn oven off and leave pastitsio inside for 10 minutes. Remove from oven and let stand for 5 minutes before serving.

Stuffed Eggplants (Little Shoes)

Melitzanes papoutsakia

Serves 3 (or 6 as an entrée)

3 × 250-g (9-oz) eggplants,
  halved lengthways

salt

⅓ cup (80 ml/3 fl oz) olive oil

1 cup (250 ml/8½ fl oz) tomato
  sauce (page 239)

1 large onion, chopped

2 cloves garlic, crushed

400 g (1 lb 2 oz) lamb
  or beef mince

1 cup chopped tomatoes

1 tablespoon tomato paste

2 tablespoons chopped
  fresh parsley

½ teaspoon ground cinnamon

½ teaspoon sugar

freshly ground black pepper

1 egg, lightly beaten

¼ teaspoon ground nutmeg

1½ cups (375 ml/12½ fl oz)
  béchamel sauce (page 247)

¾ cup grated kefalotiri

Preheat oven to 180°C (360°F). Line a baking tray with baking paper.

Sprinkle cut sides of eggplant with salt and leave for 1 hour. Rinse egg-plants under cold water and pat dry with paper towel. Place eggplants on prepared baking tray and brush cut side with half the olive oil. Bake in pre-heated oven for 30 minutes or until soft. Remove (leave oven on). Score the eggplant flesh and press down to compress it against the skin.

Pour tomato sauce into the bottom of a large baking dish and place egg-plant cases on top. Set aside. >

Heat remaining oil in a heavy-based saucepan over medium heat. Add onion and garlic and sauté until soft. Increase heat, add meat and cook, stirring, until it browns. Add tomatoes, tomato paste, parsley, cinnamon and sugar, and season with salt and pepper. Cover, reduce heat and simmer gently for 10 minutes, or until sauce thickens. Remove from heat and allow to cool.

Fill the eggplant shells with meat mixture.

Add egg and nutmeg to the warm béchamel sauce and stir to combine. Spread béchamel sauce over filled eggplants and scatter with cheese. Place tray in preheated oven and cook, uncovered, for 35–45 minutes or until golden.

Serve as an entrée or main course with salad and crusty bread.

Medium-sized zucchini can be prepared in the same way.

Lamb with Sour Cherry Sauce

Serves 4–6

1 × 1.5-kg (3 lb 5-oz) leg
of lamb, deboned and
butterflied (ask your butcher
to do this)

salt and freshly ground
black pepper

1 tablespoon dried oregano

½ cup (125 ml/4 fl oz) olive oil

SOUR CHERRY SAUCE

2 tablespoons sour cherry jam
(or any berry jam)

1 tablespoon Dijon mustard

2 tablespoons (40 g/1½ oz)
soft brown sugar

3 tablespoons (60 g/2 oz)
butter

2 tablespoons (40 ml/1½ fl oz)
freshly squeezed lemon juice

1 teaspoon ground cinnamon

salt and freshly ground
black pepper

2 tablespoons (40 ml/1½ fl oz)
tomato sauce

½ cup (125 ml/4 fl oz) beef
(or chicken) stock

Preheat oven to 180°C (360°F).

Place a wire rack in a baking dish and fill dish to a third with water. Place lamb, cut-side down, on the rack. Rub salt, pepper, oregano and oil onto fat side of lamb. Roast in preheated oven for 25 minutes.

Meanwhile, to make the sauce, place all ingredients in a saucepan over medium heat. Slowly bring to the boil, then reduce heat and simmer for about 5 minutes. >

Remove dish from oven, turn lamb over and pour half the cherry sauce onto the meat. Return to the oven and cook for a further 45–60 minutes, basting with juices from the pan every 30 minutes. When the lamb is cooked to your liking, remove from the oven and allow to stand for 5 minutes.

Serve lamb sliced, with remaining sauce drizzled on top, and accompanied with a salad and baked potatoes.

Goat Stew with Wine & Onions

Stifado katsiki

Serves 6–8

⅓ cup (80 ml/3 fl oz) olive oil

1.5 kg (3 lb 5 oz) kid meat (young goat), cut into cubes

1 tablespoon ground cinnamon

2½ tablespoons (50 g/1¾ oz) butter

2 medium-sized onions, finely chopped

4 cloves garlic, crushed

salt

2 tablespoons dried oregano

1 cup (250 ml/8½ fl oz) dry red wine

2 cups (500 ml/17 fl oz) beef stock

3 tablespoons tomato paste

⅓ cup (80 ml/3 fl oz) red-wine vinegar

2 cinnamon sticks

10 cloves

2 bay leaves

2 teaspoons sugar

freshly ground black pepper

1 kg (2 lb 3 oz) small pickling onions, peeled

200 g (7 oz) fetta cheese, crumbled (optional)

3 tablespoons chopped fresh parsley

Heat half the oil in a large heavy-based saucepan, add meat in batches and cook until browned, adding more oil as needed. Place meat in a bowl, add cinnamon and set aside.

Add remaining oil and butter to the saucepan and reduce heat to low, add onions and garlic and sauté until soft. Add 1 teaspoon salt and the oregano, and cook for about 5 minutes. >

Return meat to the pan, stir in the wine and increase heat, boiling for about 3–5 minutes. Add stock, tomato paste and vinegar and return to the boil. Add cinnamon stick, cloves, bay leaves and sugar, and season with salt and pepper. Reduce heat, cover and simmer over very low heat for about 1 hour.

Cut a cross in the base of each pickling onion and add them to the pan. Cook stew for a further 1–1½ hours, or until the meat is very tender and sauce has thickened. Discard cinnamon stick and bay leaves.

Serve scattered with fetta (if using) and garnished with parsley, with a side of steamed rice or pilafi.

Beef, lamb, pork or veal can be used instead of the goat.

Lamb-stuffed Cabbage Rolls

Makes 12

12 large cabbage leaves

1 tablespoon (20 ml/¾ fl oz) olive oil

1 medium-sized onion, chopped

1 clove garlic, crushed

500 g (1 lb 2 oz) lamb mince

800 g (1 lb 12 oz) canned chopped tomatoes

2 tablespoons chopped fresh parsley

½ cup chopped fresh mint

pinch of ground cinnamon (optional)

½ cup medium-grain rice

½ cup (125 ml/4 fl oz) tomato purée

salt and freshly ground black pepper

2½ cups (625 ml/21 fl oz) hot chicken stock

1 tablespoon (20 g/¾ oz) butter

⅓ cup (80 ml/3 fl oz) freshly squeezed lemon juice

1½ tablespoons (30 g/1 oz) butter

2 teaspoons cornflour

1 egg, separated

Blanch cabbage leaves for about 5 minutes in a large pot of boiling salted water. Drain and pat dry. Trim any thick core from the leaves and cut large leaves in half.

Heat oil in a heavy-based saucepan over medium heat. Add onion and garlic, and sauté until soft. Add meat and cook until it browns. Stir in chopped tomatoes, herbs, cinnamon (if using) and rice. Add tomato purée, salt and pepper to taste and mix very well. >

Cook for 5 minutes, then remove pot from heat and allow to cool.

Place a tablespoonful of mixture in the centre of each cabbage leaf. Fold in the sides of the leaf and roll up to enclose the filling. Repeat with remaining mixture. Place a cabbage leaf in the bottom of a clean heavy-based saucepan. Arrange the cabbage rolls, in rows, on top. Pour hot stock over rolls, dot with butter and add lemon juice. Put an ovenproof dinner plate on top of the cabbage rolls to help them keep their shape. Return saucepan to low heat and simmer rolls for about 1 hour.

Remove cabbage rolls from saucepan and discard cabbage leaf from base of pan. Simmer stock until reduced to ½ cup (125 ml/4 fl oz). In a bowl, mix cornflour with 2 teaspoons water to make a paste, stir it into the stock and simmer, stirring continuously, until stock boils and thickens slightly.

Beat egg white with an electric mixer until stiff peaks form, then beat in egg yolk and lemon juice. Slowly add reduced stock while continuing to beat. Return egg mixture to saucepan and whisk, over low heat, until warmed through. (Do not boil.) Spoon egg–lemon sauce over cabbage rolls and serve.

Tomato sauce (page 239) can be used instead of the egg–lemon sauce. Or the rolls can be served with lemon juice only. Beef or pork can be used instead of lamb.

Oven-cooked Lamb

Arni kleftiko

Serves 4

2 large desirée potatoes, peeled and sliced

1 tablespoon (20 g/¾ oz) butter

½ cup (125 ml/4 fl oz) olive oil

600 g (1 lb 5 oz) lamb backstrap fillets, diced

1 large red onion, sliced

4 garlic cloves, thinly sliced

2 large ripe tomatoes, chopped

1 tablespoon dried rosemary

1 tablespoon dried mint

juice of ½ lemon

salt and freshly ground black pepper

2 tomatoes, thickly sliced

½ cup fresh basil leaves

3 sheets filo pastry

1 tablespoon dried oregano

200 g (7 oz) fetta cheese

200 g (7 oz) butter, melted

Preheat oven to 160°C (320°F). Line a baking tray with baking paper.

Parboil potato slices in salted water until just tender (about 10 minutes). Drain.

Heat the butter and half the oil in a heavy-based saucepan over medium heat. Add lamb and onion, and sauté until onions are soft and lamb browns. Add garlic, tomatoes, rosemary, mint and lemon juice, and season with salt and pepper. Reduce heat, stir and simmer for 5 minutes. Remove saucepan from heat.

Heat remaining oil in a frying pan over medium heat. Add potatoes and cook until lightly browned. Remove potatoes with a slotted spoon and drain on paper towel. Add tomato slices to the pan and fry gently (about 1–2 minutes on each side). Remove pan from heat and season tomatoes with salt, pepper and chopped basil.

On a clean surface, lay out three sheets of filo pastry. Brush each sheet with melted butter, then layer sheets on top of each other. Cut pastry into quarters. Divide lamb, potatoes and fetta cheese evenly among each pastry square, placing mixture in the centre. Top each with two slices of tomato and a sprinkle of oregano and pepper.

Bring the edges of each pastry square up over the filling, to form pouches, pinching the top to give a frill. Brush each parcel lightly with melted butter, sprinkle with sesame seeds and place on prepared baking tray. Bake in the preheated oven for about 45 minutes, until lightly browned. Serve hot.

Lamb Livers

Sikotakia

Serves 4

500 g (1 lb 2 oz) lamb livers, trimmed of sinew and cut into strips

plain flour, seasoned with salt, pepper and oregano, for coating

3 tablespoons (60 ml/2 fl oz) olive oil

2 onions, thinly sliced

1 clove garlic, sliced

salt

1 sprig rosemary

⅓ cup (80 ml/3 fl oz) red-wine vinegar

2 tablespoons (40 g/1½ oz) butter

freshly ground black pepper

1 quantity skordalia (page 73), to serve

Dust liver strips with seasoned flour, shaking off any excess. Set aside.

Heat a third of the oil in a heavy-based saucepan over medium heat. Add onions, garlic, a pinch of salt and the rosemary. Cook for 2–3 minutes until onions are soft, then remove from pan. Heat half the remaining oil over high heat. Add the liver, in two batches, and cook for 1 minute on each side to caramelise and seal. (Do not overcook.) Remove liver from pan.

Heat remaining oil over medium heat and return onion mix to the pan. Add vinegar, butter and liver. Season with salt and pepper. Cook for about 5 minutes until heated through. Serve liver on top of skordalia, with pan juices poured over the top.

Stuffed Roasted Shoulder of Lamb

Arni yemisto

Serves 4–6

1 bunch fresh rosemary

1 bulb garlic, broken into cloves (unpeeled)

200 g (7 oz) kefalograviera cheese, chopped into small pieces

2 cloves garlic, crushed

1 cup chopped fresh basil

1 cup chopped fresh parsley

salt and freshly ground black pepper

1 × 2-kg (4 lb 6-oz) shoulder of lamb, boned

⅓ cup (60 ml/2 fl oz) olive oil

½ cup (125 ml/4 fl oz) dry white wine

150 g (5 oz) fetta cheese, crumbled (optional)

1 pomegranate (optional)

Preheat oven to 220°C (430°F).

Scatter half the rosemary and half the unpeeled garlic cloves over the bottom of a roasting dish.

In a bowl combine kefalograviera, crushed garlic, basil and parsley, and season with salt and pepper. Set aside.

Score the fat of the lamb with a sharp knife. Rub the lamb all over with olive oil and season with salt and pepper. Place lamb on a board, boned-side up, and spread over the stuffing. Roll up and tie in three or four places with string to hold in shape while cooking and place the lamb in the roasting dish on top of the rosemary and garlic. Cover lamb with remaining rosemary and garlic, and pour in wine.

Cover the lamb with baking paper, then cover dish with a double layer of aluminium foil. Place in the preheated oven and immediately turn temperature down to 160°C (320°F). Cook lamb for 3–4 hours. It is ready when the meat falls apart easily.

Serve the lamb sprinkled with fetta and pomegranate seeds (if using).

Pork Chops with Basil Sauce

Hirines brizoles

Serves 4

½ cup fresh oregano, chopped

1 clove garlic, crushed

salt and freshly ground
  black pepper

juice and grated zest of
  1 lemon

1 tablespoon (20 ml/¾ fl oz)
  olive oil

4 pork loin chops

BASIL SAUCE

1 clove garlic, chopped

1 cup chopped fresh basil

½ cup chopped roasted
  pistachio nuts

½ cup grated kefalotiri

⅓ cup (80 ml/3 fl oz) olive oil

salt and freshly ground
  black pepper

1 tablespoon (20 ml/¾ fl oz)
  freshly squeezed lemon juice

Place basil sauce ingredients in a food processor and blend well. Set aside.

In a bowl, combine oregano, garlic, 1 teaspoon salt, ½ teaspoon pepper, lemon juice and zest, and the oil. Smear the mixture over the chops and leave to stand for about 10 minutes.

Heat a frying pan or grill to medium–high heat. Cook chops for about 4 minutes on each side, until golden. (Make sure to not overcook as pork will become dry.) Leave chops to stand for 2–3 minutes, then spoon basil sauce over and serve.

Red Wine Stew with Rabbit

Kouneli stifado

Serves 4

1 × 1-kg rabbit, boned and cut into 8 pieces

1 cup (250 ml/8½ fl oz) red-wine vinegar

salt and freshly ground black pepper

2 tablespoons dried oregano

3 tablespoons (60 ml/2 fl oz) olive oil

125 g (9 oz) butter

1 medium-sized onion, sliced

4 cloves garlic, sliced

1 × 400-g (14-oz) can chopped tomatoes

1 tablespoon tomato paste

1 cup (250 ml/8½ fl oz) tomato purée

½ cup (125 ml/4 fl oz) dry red wine

1 cinnamon stick

1 sprig rosemary

1 bay leaf

1 teaspoon sugar

4 cloves

500 g (1 lb 2 oz) small pickling onions or shallots, peeled

chopped fresh flat-leaf parsley, for garnish

Combine rabbit pieces with vinegar and water in a large bowl – make sure liquid covers the rabbit. Cover bowl with cling wrap and refrigerate for 12 hours or overnight. Drain meat, rinse in plenty of cold water and pat dry.

Preheat oven to 180°C (360°F).

Rub rabbit pieces with salt, pepper and half the oregano.

Heat oil and butter in a saucepan over medium heat. Add rabbit pieces and cook until golden (about 10 minutes). Remove rabbit from pan and place in an ovenproof dish.

In the same saucepan, over medium heat, combine the sliced onion, garlic, 1 teaspoon salt and remaining oregano, and sauté until onion is soft. Add chopped tomatoes, tomato paste, tomato purée, red wine, cinnamon, rosemary, remaining oregano, bay leaf, sugar and cloves. Season with salt and pepper. Bring sauce to the boil, reduce heat and simmer for 5 minutes. Add the small onions and simmer for another 5 minutes.

Add sauce to the dish with the rabbit, and cover with a lid or a double layer of aluminium foil. Cook in the preheated oven for 2 hours until onions and rabbit are tender.

Serve garnished with parsley.

Sausages in Tomato Sauce

Sousoukakia

Serves 4–6

500 g (1 lb 2 oz) finely-
 ground beef mince

500 g (1 lb 2 oz) finely-
 ground lamb mince

2 eggs, beaten

2 cloves garlic, crushed

2 teaspoons toasted
 ground cumin

1 large onion, diced

salt and freshly ground
 black pepper

½ cup fresh breadcrumbs

2 teaspoons dried oregano

3 tablespoons (60 ml/2 fl oz)
 port

1 quantity tomato sauce
 (page 239), with 1 teaspoon
 toasted ground cumin added
 at the end

Preheat oven to 170°C (340°F). Line a baking tray with baking paper.

Combine all ingredients, except the tomato sauce, in a bowl and mix well
with your hands. Use your hands to shape the mixture into sausages about
8 cm (3 in) long and 5 cm (2 in) wide.

Place sausages on the prepared tray and bake for about 20 minutes, turning after 10 minutes. (You can prepare the tomato sauce while the sausages
are cooking.)

Add cooked sausages to the hot tomato sauce and simmer over low heat
for 30 minutes. Serve hot, with spaghetti, pilafi or fried potatoes and a green
salad.

Drunken Pork

Bekri meze

Serves 4

500 g (1 lb 12 oz) boneless
  pork loin, cut into bite-sized
  pieces

2 tablespoons Dijon mustard

⅓ cup (80 ml/3 fl oz) olive oil

1 onion, chopped

2 cloves garlic, crushed

1 cup (250 ml/8½ fl oz) sweet
  red wine (or use dry wine
  if preferred)

1 cup chopped tomatoes

1 cup (250 ml/8½ fl oz)
  tomato purée

½ teaspoon ground paprika

½ teaspoon dried oregano

¼ teaspoon ground allspice

salt and freshly ground
  black pepper

Combine pork pieces and mustard. Set aside.

Heat oil in a heavy-based frying pan over medium heat, add onion, garlic and pork, and cook, stirring frequently, until the meat is lightly browned (about 10 minutes). Stir in the wine, and increase heat to high. Cook until wine has evaporated. Add tomatoes, tomato purée, paprika, oregano and allspice. Season with salt and pepper. Reduce heat and simmer for about 20 minutes, until the meat is tender and the sauce has thickened.

Serve immediately with pilafi or steamed rice.

🔲 This dish can be served on its own as a meze.

Stuffed Roast Pork

Serves 6–8

1 × 2-kg (4½-lb) boned and
rolled pork shoulder

salt and freshly ground
black pepper

½ cup (125 ml/4 fl oz) dry
white wine

MARINADE

½ cup (125 ml/4 fl oz) olive oil

1 clove garlic, crushed

1 tablespoon Dijon mustard

1 teaspoon dried oregano

juice and grated zest of
½ orange

1 teaspoon toasted cumin
seeds, crushed

STUFFING

2 tablespoons (40 g/1½ oz)
butter

1 small leek, thinly sliced

½ cup chopped pistachio nuts

1 cup fresh breadcrumbs

1 large green apple, peeled,
cored and chopped

2 tablespoons finely chopped
fresh flat-leaf parsley

2 tablespoons (40 ml/1½ fl oz)
freshly squeezed lemon

salt and freshly ground
black pepper

To make the marinade, combine all ingredients in a bowl and mix well. Rub
marinade over pork and refrigerate for about 1 hour.

Preheat oven to 220°C (430°F). Lightly grease a baking dish. >

To make the stuffing, heat butter in a small saucepan over low heat. Add leek and nuts, and cook over low heat, stirring occasionally, for 5 minutes, until the onion is softened and the nuts are lightly browned. Add breadcrumbs, apple and parsley and cook, stirring continuously, for 5 minutes. Stir in the lemon juice, season with salt and pepper, then remove pan from heat.

Place marinated pork in the prepared baking dish. Untie the pork and unroll, spread stuffing evenly over the meat, then reroll and tie securely with kitchen string. Brush the pork with any leftover marinade.

Roast the pork for about 30 minutes, or until the skin starts to brown. Reduce the oven temperature to 180°C (360°F) and roast for a further 1½ hours, or until cooked through.

Transfer pork to a serving dish and keep warm. Add wine to the roasting pan and stir over medium heat for about 3 minutes. Reduce heat and simmer gravy until slightly reduced.

Serve pork with the gravy.

Lamb, Eggplant & Capsicum Skewers

Serves 6

3 red capsicums

4 baby eggplant, cut
   lengthways into thin slices

½ cup (125 ml/4 fl oz) olive oil

salt

1 tablespoon dried oregano

750 g (1 lb 10 oz) lamb
   backstrap, cut into 36 pieces

2 cloves garlic, finely chopped

juice of 1 lemon

freshly ground black pepper

12 bamboo skewers, soaked
   in water for 30 minutes

warmed pita bread, to serve

tzatziki (page 37), to serve

Heat a grill or barbecue plate to hot. Cook capsicums, turning occasionally, until blackened and blistered (6–8 minutes). Place in a bowl, cover with cling wrap and allow to cool (this will loosen skins). Brush eggplant slices with oil, season with salt and oregano, and grill for 2–3 minutes on each side.

Peel capsicums, remove seeds and cut each into about 12 strips.

In a bowl combine, garlic, lemon juice and remaining oil. Season with salt and pepper. Alternately thread three pieces each of capsicum, eggplant and lamb onto each skewer. Brush skewers with garlic and lemon dressing.

Heat grill or barbecue to medium–hot and cook skewers for 2–3 minutes on each side or until meat is just cooked through. Serve immediately with warmed pita bread and tzatziki.

Pork & Quince Bake

Serves 4–6

140 g (5 oz) butter

3 tablespoons (60 ml/2 fl oz) olive oil

1 kg (2 lb 3 oz) pork shoulder, cubed

1 large onion, finely chopped

½ cup (125 ml/4 fl oz) red wine

1 cup (250 ml/8½ fl oz) beef stock

1 thin strip orange zest

1 cinnamon stick

1 × 400-g (14-oz) can chopped tomatoes

¼ teaspoon mixed spice

salt and freshly ground black pepper

1 kg (2 lb 3 oz) quinces, peeled, cored, sliced into wedges and sprinkled with freshly squeezed lemon juice

2 tablespoons honey

Preheat oven to 180°C (360°F).

Heat 100 g (3½ oz) of the butter with the oil in a heavy-based saucepan over medium heat. Add pork and cook until it browns (about 8 minutes). Add onion and fry gently until soft. Add remaining ingredients (except quince and honey), season with salt and pepper, reduce heat and simmer for 5 minutes.

Transfer pork mixture to an ovenproof dish, cover with aluminium foil and bake in the oven for 1 hour.

Melt remaining butter in a saucepan over medium heat. Add quince and cook, stirring occasionally, until lightly browned (about 5 minutes). Add honey and cook, stirring continuously, for 5 minutes.

Remove pork from oven and pour the honey and quince sauce over. Baste pork with pan juices, re-cover and cook for a further 30 minutes. Baste pork again and cook uncovered for 10 minutes. Serve hot.

Eggplant Moussaka

Serves 8

1.5 kg potatoes, cut into
5-mm (¼-in) slices

1 cup (250 ml/8½ fl oz)
olive oil

salt

2½ teaspoons dried oregano

1 kg eggplant, cut into
5-mm (¼-in) slices

1 large onion, chopped

2 cloves garlic, crushed

1 kg lamb (or beef) mince

800 g (1 lb 12 oz) canned
tomatoes

3 tablespoons tomato paste

½ cup (125 ml/4 fl oz) red wine

1 teaspoon sugar

1 teaspoon ground allspice

1 teaspoon ground cinnamon

freshly ground black pepper

½ cup grated kefalotiri

1 cup grated parmesan cheese

½ tablespoon ground nutmeg

1 quantity béchamel sauce
(page 247)

Preheat oven to 180°C (360°F). Line two baking trays with baking paper. Grease a 35-cm × 25-cm (14-in × 10-in) baking dish.

Parboil the potato slices in salted water for about 10 minutes. Drain.

Place potatoes on one of the prepared baking trays. Brush slices with oil and sprinkle with salt and 1 teaspoon oregano. Bake, turning once, until golden-brown on both sides (about 15 minutes). Set aside.

Arrange slices of eggplant in a single layer on the other baking tray. Brush with oil and sprinkle with salt and 1 teaspoon oregano. Grill on both sides until lightly browned (about 10 minutes).

Heat remaining oil in a heavy-based saucepan over medium heat. Add onion, garlic, ½ teaspoon salt and ½ teaspoon oregano, and sauté until onion is soft. Add mince and cook, stirring, until meat is browned. Add chopped tomatoes, tomato paste, wine, sugar, allspice and cinnamon. Season to taste with salt and pepper. Reduce heat and simmer, uncovered, for 40 minutes.

You can make the béchamel while the meat sauce is cooking. Add 1 cup of kefalotiri to the béchamel.

Place a layer of potato slices on the bottom of the prepared baking dish and follow with a layer of eggplant slices. Spread half the meat sauce over the top, then sprinkle with a third of the parmesan cheese and a third of the nutmeg. Add another layer of potato and eggplant slices, pour the remaining meat sauce over, sprinkle with half the remaining parmesan and nutmeg, and top with the béchamel sauce. Sprinkle the top of the moussaka with the remaining parmesan and nutmeg.

Bake in the preheated oven for 45 minutes or until golden-brown. Remove from oven and allow to stand for about 10 minutes before serving.

Lamb Cutlets Stuffed with Olives & Fetta

Serves 6–8

12 good-quality lamb cutlets, French trimmed

130 g (4½ oz) fetta cheese

2 tablespoons chopped fresh flat-leaf parsley

2 tablespoons chopped fresh basil

2 tablespoons (40 ml/1½ fl oz) olive oil, plus extra for brushing

1 clove garlic, crushed

6 kalamata olives, pitted and finely chopped

salt and freshly ground black pepper

2 tablespoons fresh or dried oregano

lemon wedges, to serve

Using a sharp knife, make a pocket in each cutlet by making a slit in the side (without cutting all the way through), then using your finger make a hole.

Combine remaining ingredients in a bowl. Stuff a teaspoonful of mixture into the pocket of each cutlet. Lightly brush lamb with oil on both sides, and season with salt, pepper and oregano.

Heat a grill or barbecue to medium–hot or heat a tablespoon of oil in a non-stick frying pan over high heat. Cook cutlets in batches for about 3–4 minutes on each side.

Season with salt and pepper and serve with lemon wedges and a crisp salad.

Easter Lamb on the Spit

Serves 15–20

salt
freshly ground black pepper
1 cup dried oregano
1 × 12-kg (26½-lb) whole lamb
8–10 lemons
1 cup (250 ml/8½ fl oz) olive oil

Combine ½ cup salt, 2 tablespoons pepper and ½ cup oregano in a bowl.

On a clean, large surface, lay out the lamb and rub it, both inside and out, with the spice mix.

Mix together ½ cup salt, ½ cup oregano, 1 cup olive oil, 2 tablespoons pepper and the juice of 6 lemons. Set marinade aside.

Rub the long metal spike attachment of the spit, or *souvla*, with lemon juice (this helps clean and sterilise it).

Pass the spike between the hind legs of the lamb, through the stomach cavity and out through the chest cavity next to the neck. The lamb's spine should be straight along the line of the spit. Then tie the underside of the lamb together with cooking string.

Tie the legs, neck and forearms down tight (if your spit comes with clamps, use these and secure it with wire as well). Then, depending on the type of spit you are using, attach the spike accordingly.

Cook lamb for about 30 minutes, until it has warmed through (it will begin to sweat). From this point onwards, baste the lamb with the marinade every 30 minutes, to stop it from browning too much and drying out. Total cooking time should be 4–5 hours. After 3 hours you may need to wrap the middle part of the lamb in foil if it is starting to get too dark – this part of the lamb tends to cook a lot faster than the shoulders and legs.

To achieve a crispy skin, do not baste in the last hour of cooking. The meat is ready when it falls away easily from the bones. (You can ask your butcher to give you an estimate of how long the lamb will take to cook.)

The easiest spit to use for this recipe is a large, electric powered gas or charcoal fired spit. These can be readily hired or purchased. You can also ask your butcher to attach the lamb to the spike if you are unsure of how it should be done.

Sweets

There is a large variety of delicious Greek sweets that are traditionally served with coffee or when visitors drop by. Most Greek pastries and confections are flavoured with spices such as cinnamon, mahlepi, cloves and nutmeg. Fresh seasonal fruit is very popular to serve after dinner.

< Almond Shortbread (page 180)

Almond Shortbread

Kourambiedes

Makes about 30

250 g (9 oz) softened butter

½ cup (80 g/3 oz) icing sugar, plus extra for dusting

1 egg yolk

1 tablespoon (20 ml/¾ fl oz) Metaxa brandy (optional)

110 g (4 oz) toasted slivered almond, roughly chopped

1 × 25-g (⅞-oz) packet vanillin sugar

2 cups (300 g/10½ oz) self-raising flour

½ cup (75 g/2½ oz) plain flour, plus extra for dusting

30 cloves (optional)

Preheat oven to 160°C (320°F). Line a baking tray with baking paper.

Using an electric mixer, beat butter and icing sugar until light and fluffy. Stir in egg yolk, brandy (if using), almonds and vanillin sugar. Gradually add sifted flours until well combined.

Knead mixture on a floured bench until it forms a soft dough that isn't sticky. (If it is too sticky add a little more plain flour.)

Take small pieces of dough and shape into crescents. Space out on prepared tray and place a whole clove (if using) in the centre of each shortbread. Bake in the oven for 20–25 minutes, turning tray after about 10 minutes.

Remove biscuits from the oven and allow to cool slightly. Dust with icing sugar until completely covered.

Store in an airtight container for up to 3 weeks.

Kourambiedes are the national biscuits of Greece and are traditionally served at Christmas time. The clove symbolises the spices brought to the Child Christ by the three wise men.

Figs in Syrup

50 small unripe green figs
4 cups (880 g/1 lb 15 oz) caster sugar
juice of ½ lemon
1 strip lemon zest

Wash figs and trim stems. Place in a large saucepan over medium heat, cover with water and bring to the boil, then reduce heat and simmer for 10 minutes. Drain and rinse figs then return them to the saucepan, cover with warm water and bring to the boil. Reduce heat and simmer for 10 minutes. Repeat process once more. The figs should now be tender. Spread figs out on paper towel to dry.

Add remaining ingredients to a saucepan over medium heat and add 1 L (34 fl oz) water. Bring to the boil, then reduce to a simmer. Add figs to the saucepan and simmer for 10 minutes, skimming scum from the surface if necessary. Remove pan from heat, cover and leave overnight at room temperature.

Bring pan slowly to the boil over low heat and simmer until syrup becomes thick (about 10–15 minutes). Take pan off heat and cool. Transfer figs and syrup to sterilised jars. Store in a cool place for up to six months. Always serve at room temperature.

Walnut Cake

Karidopita

Serves 8–10

250 g (9 oz) softened butter

1 cup (220 g/8 oz) caster sugar

1 tablespoon grated orange zest

4 eggs, separated

1 cup (150 g/5 oz) plain flour

1 cup (150 g/5 oz) fine semolina

4 teaspoons baking powder

1 teaspoon ground cinnamon

1 × 25-g (⅞-oz) packet vanillin sugar

½ cup (125 ml/4 fl oz) full-cream milk

2 cups coarsely chopped walnuts

SYRUP

2 cups (440 g/15½ oz) caster sugar

1 cinnamon stick

juice of ½ orange

3 slices thinly peeled orange zest

Preheat the oven to 170°C (340°F). Grease a 33-cm × 23-cm (13-in × 9-in) baking dish.

Cream butter and sugar with grated orange zest until light and fluffy. Add egg yolks, one at a time, beating well.

In a bowl, mix together the sifted flour, semolina, baking powder, cinnamon and vanillin sugar. >

Fold a third of the flour mix into the creamed mixture, followed by a third of the milk. Fold in half the remaining flour and then half the remaining milk. Lastly, fold in remaining flour and milk. Gently mix in the walnuts.

Beat egg whites until stiff. Fold into the batter using a metal spoon.

Pour mixture into the prepared dish and bake for 45 minutes or until cooked through. (Test with a metal skewer – if it comes out clean, the cake is ready.)

To make the syrup, place all ingredients in a heavy-based saucepan with 2 cups (500 ml/17 fl oz) water and bring to the boil over high heat. Once syrup boils, reduce to medium heat and simmer for 10 minutes.

Score a diamond pattern into the top of the hot cake and pour hot syrup over. Serve the cake hot or cold.

Yoghurt Cake

Yiaourtopita

Serves 8–10

1 cup (250 ml/8½ fl oz) oil

1½ cups (330 g/11½ oz)
  caster sugar

grated zest of ½ lemon

5 eggs, separated

3 cups (450 g/16 oz)
  self-raising flour

1 × 25-g (⅞-oz) packet vanillin
  sugar

1 cup (250 ml/8½ fl oz)
  Greek-style yoghurt

icing sugar, for dusting

Preheat oven to 180°C (360°F). Grease a 23-cm (9-in) round cake tin or a 25-cm × 35-cm (10-in × 14-in) cake tin.

In a food processor combine oil, caster sugar and lemon zest until light, add egg yolks and beat well. Sift together the flour and vanillin sugar. Add dry ingredients alternately with yoghurt.

Beat egg whites until stiff peaks form, and gently fold into batter.

Pour mixture into cake tin and cook in the oven for about 50–60 minutes or until cooked (a skewer inserted into the centre of the cake should come out clean).

Turn cake out onto a wire rack to cool. Dust with icing sugar before serving with cream or ice-cream.

Semolina-filled Parcels

Bougatsa

Makes 30

1 L (34 fl oz) full-cream milk

1 × 25-g (⅞-oz) packet
vanillin sugar

1 cup (220 g/8 oz) caster sugar

1 cup (150 g/5 oz) fine
semolina

6 eggs, whisked

340 g (12 oz) softened butter

1 × 375-g (13-oz) packet
filo pastry

icing sugar and ground
cinnamon, for dusting

Preheat oven to 170°C (340°F). Line a baking tray with baking paper.

Combine milk, sugars and semolina in a saucepan over low heat. Add eggs and stir until smooth and thick. Remove from heat and stir in 220 g (8 oz) of the butter. Set aside and let cool.

Melt remaining butter. On a clean surface, lay three sheets of filo on top of each other, brushing between each layer with melted butter. Cut pastry lengthways into three strips. Place a teaspoonful of the semolina custard along the short edge closest to you, leaving a 1 cm (⅜ in) border. Brush the filo with butter, then fold pastry over the custard, fold in the edges, then roll up into a cigar shape. Repeat with remaining mixture and filo. Place parcels on prepared baking tray and brush tops with melted butter. Bake for 20–30 minutes until slight coloured. Turn off oven and leave parcels inside, with door slightly ajar, for 15 minutes. Remove parcels from oven, allow to cool slightly before dusting with icing sugar and cinnamon. Serve warm or cold.

Sour Cherries in Syrup

Visino glyko

Makes 1 kg

**1 kg (2 lb 3 oz) sour cherries,
  pips removed but kept whole**

1 kg (2 lb 3 oz) caster sugar

juice of 1 large lemon

1 cinnamon stick

Layer cherries and sugar in a saucepan. Add 2 cups (500 ml/17 fl oz) water and bring to the boil. Boil for 25 minutes, stirring often, removing any scum from the surface. Remove from the heat and stand at room temperature for 12 hours.

Add lemon juice and cinnamon stick to the cold syrup and bring to the boil over medium heat. Reduce heat, simmer and continue to cook until syrup is thick. Test the syrup by dropping a little onto a cold saucer – if the drops do not spread then it is ready. Transfer to sterilised jars and seal once cold.

Serve a few cherries with syrup as a sweet accompaniment to Greek coffee.

🄿 Sour cherries in a jar can be purchased from Continental delis.

🄿 To make a refreshing summer drink, mix 1 tablespoon of syrup with iced water or soda water in a tall glass.

Baked Halva

Serves 6–8

½ cup (75 g/2½ oz) plain flour

2 teaspoons baking powder

1 × 25-g (⅞-oz) packet vanillin sugar

1 teaspoon ground cinnamon (or nutmeg)

pinch of salt

2 cups (300 g/10½ oz) fine semolina

1 cup toasted almonds, chopped

200 g (7 oz) softened butter

1 cup (220 g/8 oz) caster sugar

4 eggs

¾ cup (180 ml/6 fl oz) orange juice

grated zest of ½ orange (optional)

SPICED SYRUP

1 slice grated orange zest

3 cups sugar

1 cinnamon stick

4 cloves

Preheat oven to 180°C (360°F). Grease a 23-cm (9-in) round baking dish.

In a bowl sift together flour, baking powder, vanillin sugar, ground cinnamon and salt. Add semolina and nuts, and mix well.

Cream butter and caster sugar in a food processor until light and fluffy. Add beaten eggs one at a time. Add combined orange juice and zest alternately with dry ingredients, beating well after each addition, until smooth. >

Transfer mixture to the prepared baking dish and bake in the oven for about 45 minutes.

Meanwhile, place all syrup ingredients in a saucepan with 3 cups (750 ml/ 25 fl oz) water. Bring to the boil over medium heat, then reduce heat and simmer for about 5 minutes.

As soon as halva is ready, pour syrup over, then cut into square- or triangle-shaped serving pieces. Allow to cool slightly before serving with good-quality ice-cream.

Baklava

Serves 8–10

1 × 375-g (13-oz) packet
filo pastry

NUT FILLING

2½ cups coarsely chopped
roasted almonds

2½ cups coarsely chopped
roasted walnuts

1 cup chopped pistachio nuts

3 teaspoons ground cinnamon

½ teaspoon mixed spice

½ teaspoon ground nutmeg

1 cup (150 g/5 oz) soft brown
sugar

200 g (7 oz) melted butter,
for brushing

30 cloves (optional)

LEMON SYRUP

2 cups (440 g/15½ oz)
caster sugar

1 cinnamon stick

1 tablespoon honey

1 thin strip lemon zest

2 tablespoons (40 ml/1½ fl oz)
freshly squeezed lemon juice

Preheat oven to 180°C (360°F). Grease a 35-cm × 25-cm baking dish.

Combine all filling ingredients in a bowl.

Lay eight sheets of filo on top of each other, brushing with melted butter between each layer. Fit pastry into base of prepared dish and sprinkle evenly with a third of the nut mixture. Repeat this procedure with two more layers of pastry and nuts. Top the last nut layer with 12 sheets of filo, brushing with butter between each layer before placing the pastry stack into the dish.

With a sharp knife score the top pastry layer into small diamond shapes. If desired, insert a clove in the centre of each piece. Bake for about 30–40 minutes or until golden-brown.

Meanwhile, make the syrup by placing all the ingredients into a saucepan with 2 cups (500 mls/17 fl oz) water. Bring to the boil then reduce heat and simmer for about 10 minutes.

When baklava is ready take it out of the oven. Ladle the hot syrup carefully over the hot baklava. Leave the baklava to absorb the syrup and cool completely. Serve at room temperature. (Do not store in the refrigerator.)

Copenhagen Almond Sweet

Copenhayi

Serves 8–10

4 eggs, separated

½ cup (110 g/4 oz) caster sugar

⅓ cup (80 ml/3 fl oz) orange juice

1 teaspoon ground cinnamon

1 teaspoon baking powder

1 cup coarsely ground toasted almonds

¼ teaspoon ground cloves

1 cup (50 g/1¾ oz) fresh breadcrumbs, lightly toasted

¼ teaspoon salt

1 × 375-g (13-oz) packet filo pastry

200 g butter, melted

ORANGE SYRUP

2 cups (440 g/15½ oz) caster sugar

juice of ½ orange (125 ml/4 fl oz)

1 strip orange zest

1 cinnamon stick

Preheat the oven to 170°C (340°F). Grease a 23-cm × 33-cm (9-in × 13-in) baking dish.

Beat egg yolks with the sugar until mixture is very thick, then add orange juice, cinnamon, baking powder, almonds, cloves and breadcrumbs.

Beat egg whites with salt until stiff. Fold into almond mixture. >

Line the baking dish with half the filo pastry sheets, brushing each sheet liberally with melted butter before placing the next on top. Spread almond mixture evenly into dish and place the remaining sheets of (buttered) pastry on top. Score top into serving pieces with a sharp knife.

Bake for about 45 minutes, until golden.

To make the syrup, place all ingredients in a heavy-based saucepan with 1 cup (250ml/8½ fl oz) water and bring to the boil, then reduce heat and simmer for 10 minutes. Remove from heat.

Pour the hot syrup over the pastry dish and allow to cool.

When cold, cut along the scored lines. Serve at room tempature.

🏛 This almond sweet was created in honour of King George I of the Hellenes (who was a Danish prince before he became king).

Halva

1 cup (220 g/8 oz) caster sugar	1 cup (150 g/5 oz) semolina
1 cinnamon stick	1 teaspoon ground cinnamon
grated zest of ½ lemon	¼ teaspoon ground cloves
4 cloves	2 tablespoons honey
125 g (4½ oz) butter	1 cup toasted walnuts, crushed

Dissolve sugar in 3 cups (750 ml/25 fl oz) water and bring to the boil. Add cinnamon stick, lemon zest and cloves, simmer for 5 minutes, then set aside.

Heat butter in a saucepan over medium heat until brown. Stir in the semolina and half of the nuts. Add ground spices and stir constantly until semolina is golden-brown (about 15 minutes). Remove from heat.

Remove cinnamon stick and cloves from syrup and pour syrup into semolina mix, stirring constantly. Add honey, return to low heat and cook for a couple of minutes, stirring with a wooden spoon, until it thickens.

Remove halva from heat and spoon into a serving dish or greased cake mould (if using a cake mould, sprinkle some walnuts inside the mould first). Sprinkle top with the crushed walnuts. Allow to cool, then cut into diamond shapes and serve with coffee.

Honey & Walnut Biscuits

Melomakarona

Makes 25–30

4 cups (600 g/1 lb 5 oz) plain flour

½ teaspoon bicarbonate of soda

1 teaspoon baking powder

⅔ cup (150 g/5 oz) caster sugar

2 teaspoons ground cinnamon, plus extra for dusting

½ teaspoon ground cloves

zest of 1 orange

1 cup (250 ml/8½ fl oz) oil

¾ cup (180 ml/6 fl oz) freshly squeezed orange juice

3 tablespoons (60 ml/2 fl oz) Metaxa brandy (or any other brandy)

2 cups roughly chopped walnuts

ORANGE SYRUP

2 cups (440 g/15½ oz) caster sugar

2 tablespoons Greek honey

1 cinnamon stick

4 cloves

1 thin strip orange zest

3 tablespoons (60 ml/2 fl oz) orange juice

Preheat oven to 170°C (340°F). Line a baking tray with baking paper.

Mix sifted flour with all other dry ingredients (except nuts) and the orange zest.

In a separate bowl mix together the oil, orange juice and brandy. >

Combine the liquid and dry ingredients and mix well. Turn dough out onto a clean floured surface and knead lightly. Roll tablespoonfuls of mixture into ovals. Place on the prepared baking tray, leaving room for spreading. Bake in the oven for 20–25 minutes.

Meanwhile, to make the syrup, place all ingredients in a saucepan with 2 cups (500 ml/17 fl oz) water. Bring to the boil over medium heat, then reduce heat and simmer for about 5 minutes, skimming any scum that rises to the surface. Set aside.

When biscuits are ready, transfer to a baking dish and pour the hot syrup over to cover. Leave biscuits in the syrup for 2–3 hours, turning often to coat them evenly.

Arrange biscuits on a serving platter and sprinkle with chopped walnuts and cinnamon, and drizzle with a little extra syrup.

Only those biscuits which are to be served immediately should be dipped in syrup – store remainder in an airtight container and dip in syrup when required.

Honeyed Goat's Cheese & Fig Parcels

Makes 8

- 400 g (14 oz) soft goat's cheese, crumbled
- 3 tablespoons honey, plus extra for garnish
- 1 tablespoon (20 ml/¾ fl oz) orange-blossom water (optional)
- 8 sheets filo pastry
- 150 g (5 oz) butter, melted
- 8 dried figs, sliced
- ½ cup chopped walnuts, plus extra for garnish
- ½ cup toasted chopped almonds
- ground cinnamon, for dusting

Preheat oven to 170°C (340°F).

Combine goat's cheese and honey in a bowl with the orange-blossom water (if using).

On a clean work surface, lay out four sheets of filo pastry on top of each other, brushing between each layer with melted butter. Cut pastry stack in half vertically, then in half horizontally to make four squares. Repeat to make four more pastry squares.

Place a tablespoonful of the cheese mixture in the centre of each pastry square. Arrange a sliced fig on top of each and place 1 teaspoon walnuts on the figs. Bring the sides of the pastry up over the cheese filling to make a parcel and pinch together, leaving a little frill at the top. >

Brush parcels with melted butter and bake in the oven for about 20 minutes or until golden-brown. Remove from oven, drizzle with honey, sprinkle with cinnamon and chopped nuts, and serve.

🔲 Fresh figs can be used instead of dried figs.

Kataifi with Cream

Serves 8–10

1 × 375-g (13-oz) packet
kataifi pastry

½ cup roughly chopped
toasted pistachio nuts

125 g (4½ oz) butter, melted

½ cup roughly chopped
toasted almonds

ORANGE SYRUP

2 cups (440 g/15½ fl oz)
caster sugar

1 cinnamon stick

3 strips orange peel

2 tablespoons (40 ml/1½ fl oz)
orange juice

CREAM FILLING

½ cup (110 g/4 oz)
caster sugar

½ cup (75 g/2½ oz) plain flour

1 L (34 fl oz) milk

4 egg yolks

1 vanilla pod, seeds scraped

1 × 25-g (⅞-oz) packet vanillin
sugar

1 tablespoon grated orange
zest

100 g (3½ oz) butter, diced

Preheat oven to 180°C (360°F). Grease a 30-cm × 24-cm (12-in × 9½-in)
baking dish with butter.

Pull kataifi pastry apart and mix pistachio nuts into it. Spread pastry over
the base of the prepared baking dish and pour melted butter over it. Bake
in the oven for 20–30 minutes, or until golden-brown.

To make the syrup, place all ingredients in a saucepan with 2 cups (500 ml/ 17 fl oz) water and bring to the boil. Reduce heat and simmer for about 10 minutes.

Pour the syrup over the kataifi and sprinkle with half the chopped almonds.

To make the cream filling, place all ingredients, except the butter, in a saucepan and stir continuously over low heat until boiling, then add butter and whisk until combined. Remove from heat, pour the cream over the kataifi, and sprinkle with remaining almonds. Cover dish and refrigerate until set (about 2 hours).

Slice the kataifi and serve with fresh strawberries.

Easter Cookies

Koulouria

Makes 7–8 dozen

2 cups (300 g/10½ oz)
plain flour

6 cups (900 g/2 lb) self-raising
flour

500 g (1 lb 2 oz) softened butter

2 cups (440 g/15½ oz)
caster sugar

3 eggs, at room temperature

2 × 25-g (⅞-oz) packets
vanillin sugar

grated zest of 1 orange

1 teaspoon ground cinnamon

1½ cups (375 ml /13 fl oz)
freshly squeezed orange
juice

1 lightly beaten egg

1 cup toasted almond flakes
(optional)

½ cup sesame seeds (optional)

Preheat oven to 160°C (320°F). Line a baking tray with baking paper.

Sift flours together. In a separate bowl, cream butter and sugar until light and fluffy. Add eggs, vanillin sugar, zest and cinnamon. Add sifted flours alternately with orange juice until too hard for beaters to mix. Empty dough onto a floured bench and knead for 2–3 minutes. Let dough rest for 30 minutes.

Take small pieces of dough and roll into snakes about 1 cm (⅜ in) wide and 35 cm (14 in) long. Fold each snake in half and twist, then join ends to form a small ring. Alternatively, form snakes into pretzel shapes. Arrange biscuits on baking tray, brush with egg and sprinkle with almonds, or sesame seeds (if using). Bake in the oven for about 25 minutes or until golden-brown.

New Year's Cake

Vasilopita

Serves 8–10

250 g (9 oz) softened butter

1½ cups (330 g/11½ oz) caster sugar

1 tablespoon (20 ml/¾ fl oz) vanilla extract

grated zest of 1 orange

6 eggs, separated

1 cup (250 ml/8½ fl oz) orange juice

3 cups (450 g/1 lb) self-raising flour

icing sugar, for dusting

ORANGE BRANDY SYRUP

1½ cups (375 ml/12½ fl oz) orange juice

1 strip orange zest

1½ cups (330 g/11½ oz) caster sugar

1 tablespoon honey

1 tablespoon (20 ml/¾ fl oz) brandy

1 cinnamon stick

NUT TOPPING

½ cup pistachio nuts

½ cup chopped toasted walnuts

½ cup toasted almond slivers

3 tablespoons (60 g/2 oz) soft brown sugar

1 cinnamon stick

Preheat oven to 170°C (340°F). Line a 23-cm (9-in) cake tin with baking paper.

Cream butter and sugar until light and fluffy, then add vanilla, orange zest, and egg yolks. Beat well. Add a third of the orange juice followed by a third of the flour. Mix well. Continue to add juice and flour alternately.

Beat egg whites until stiff peaks form, then fold into cake batter.

Wrap a gold or silver coin in aluminium foil and add to the mixture. Pour the cake mix into the prepared cake tin and bake for 50–60 minutes. (If cake starts to become too dark while cooking, cover with foil or lower heat slightly.)

To make the syrup, place all ingredients in a heavy-based saucepan and bring to the boil over high heat. Reduce heat and simmer for about 8 minutes.

Combine topping ingredients in a bowl.

Remove cake from oven, sprinkle topping over and pour syrup slowly over the cake. When the cake cools, dust with icing sugar and serve.

Vasilopita is served at midnight as the new year starts. The cake is cut by the head of the household, who makes a sign of the cross over the cake before it is cut. Whoever ends up with the slice of cake containing the coin will have good luck and fortune in the New Year.

Nut-filled Kataifi Rolls

Makes 14

1½ cups chopped toasted
walnuts, plus extra for
garnish

1½ cups chopped toasted
almonds, plus extra for
garnish

½ cup (90 g/3 oz) soft
brown sugar

1 teaspoon grated orange zest
(optional)

2 teaspoons ground cinnamon,
plus extra for garnish

¼ teaspoon ground cloves

½ cup (125 ml/4 fl oz)
orange juice

1 × 375-g (13-oz) packet
kataifi pastry

300 g (10½ oz) butter, melted

LEMON SYRUP

3 cups (660 g/1 lb 7 oz)
caster sugar

½ cup (150 g/5 oz) honey

2 tablespoons (40 ml/1½ fl oz)
freshly squeezed lemon juice

2 strips lemon zest

1 cinnamon stick

Preheat oven to 180°C (360°F). Grease a large baking dish.

In a bowl combine nuts, brown sugar, orange zest, cinnamon and cloves.
Add orange juice and mix well. Pull the kataifi pastry apart and divide into
fourteen portions.

Place a heaped tablespoonful of the nut mixture on each kataifi portion and
roll up loosely. Repeat with remaining nut mixture and pastry.

Place kataifi rolls side by side in the prepared baking dish. Pour the melted butter evenly over the kataifi rolls and bake them in the oven for 45 minutes or until golden.

Meanwhile, to make the syrup, place all ingredients in a saucepan with 2 cups (500 ml/17 fl oz) water. Bring to the boil over medium heat, reduce heat and simmer for 10 minutes.

Remove kataifi rolls from oven. Allow to cool slightly then pour hot syrup over them. Leave rolls to stand until all the syrup has been absorbed. Garnish with chopped nuts and cinnamon and serve at room temperature.

Oranges in Syrup

Glyko portokali

Makes 48

6 large oranges

48 toothpicks

**3 cups (660 g/1 lb 7 oz)
caster sugar**

juice of ½ lemon

2 strips lemon zest

1 cinnamon stick (optional)

Lightly grate the zest from each orange and discard. Score lengthways into eight segments and then remove the peel. Keep peel segments and discard orange flesh.

Roll up each piece of peel and gently push a toothpick through to secure. Place rolls in a saucepan, cover with cold water and bring to the boil. Drain immediately. Repeat this process twice more to help remove the bitterness from the peel.

Cover rolls with cold water again and boil gently until tender (about 45 minutes). Drain and place on a tray to dry. Bring sugar and 3 cups (750 ml/25 fl oz) water to the boil, add lemon juice and zest, and boil for 5 minutes. Add orange-peel rolls and boil for 10 minutes, skimming froth when necessary. Remove from heat, cover and leave rolls overnight in the syrup. >

Bring to the boil again and cook gently for 50 minutes or until syrup is thick when tested (drip a little syrup onto a cold plate – if drops don't spread, syrup is ready).

Leave the syrup to cool, then remove toothpicks from the rolls and transfer to sterilised jars, making sure they are covered by the syrup. Seal jars and store in a cool place.

Serve at room temperature.

卍 Grapefruits or lemons can be substituted for the oranges.

Rice Pudding

Rizogalo

Serves 4

½ cup short-grain rice

pinch of salt

3½ cups (875 ml/30 fl oz) milk, plus extra

½ cup (110 g/4 oz) caster sugar

1 vanilla bean, seeds scraped

5-cm (2-in) strip orange zest

2 egg yolks

2 tablespoons (30 g/1 oz) cornflour

ground cinnamon, for dusting

Place rice in a saucepan over medium heat with 2 cups (500 ml/17 fl oz) water and the salt. Bring to the boil, stir, then lower heat and simmer for 15 minutes until liquid is absorbed. Add milk, sugar, vanilla seeds and orange zest, then stir continuously over low–medium heat for 15–20 minutes, until rice is tender.

Blend egg yolks with the cornflour and a little cold milk until well mixed. Mix about ½ cup of the rice into the egg and cornflour mixture, then return to the saucepan with the rice. Stir rice mixture gently over low heat, just long enough for mixture to thicken.

Remove orange zest. Spoon rice pudding into serving bowls and sprinkle with cinnamon. Serve hot or cold.

This pudding is delicious served with sour cherries in syrup (page 190).

Semolina Custard Slice

Galaktoboureko

Serves 8–10

5 eggs

1 cup (220 g/8 oz) caster sugar

1 cup (150 g/5 oz) fine semolina

1 L (34 fl oz) full-cream milk

grated zest of ½ lemon (optional)

1 × 25-g (⅞-oz) packet vanillin sugar

1 vanilla bean, seeds scraped

1 cinnamon stick

3 tablespoons (60 g/2 oz) butter

1 × 375-g (13-oz) packet filo pastry

150 g (5 oz) butter, melted

icing sugar, for dusting (optional)

ground cinnamon, for dusting (optional)

LEMON SYRUP

2 cups (440 g/15½ oz) caster sugar

juice and peeled zest of ½ lemon

1 cinnamon stick

Preheat the oven to 170°C (340°F). Grease a 23-cm × 30-cm (9-in × 12-in) baking dish with butter.

Beat the eggs with the caster sugar in a heavy-based saucepan. Add semolina, milk, lemon zest (if using), vanillin sugar, vanilla seeds and cinnamon stick. Cook over a low heat, stirring continuously, until mixture thickens. Remove from heat and add butter. Cover with baking paper (to prevent a skin forming) and set aside to cool. >

Layer eight sheets of filo pastry in the baking dish, brushing between the sheets with melted butter. Pour custard mixture over the pastry and top with remaining filo pastry sheets, each brushed with melted butter. Brush the top of last sheet with melted butter, then score with a sharp knife, either into square or rectangle serving shapes. Place in the preheated oven and cook for about 45 minutes, until pastry is golden-brown and custard is set.

Meanwhile, to make the syrup, place all ingredients in a saucepan with 2 cups (500 ml/ 17 fl oz) water over medium heat. Bring to the boil, reduce heat and simmer for about 10 minutes.

Remove baking dish from the oven, pour hot syrup over the top of the slice, then allow to stand until cool. Dust with icing sugar and/or cinnamon (if using) and serve.

Greek Doughnuts

Loukoumades

Makes about 30

1 × 7-g (¼-oz) packet dry yeast

2 cups (500 ml/17 fl oz)
warm water

2 tablespoons (30 g/1 oz)
caster sugar

1 × 25-g (⅞-oz) packet
vanillin sugar

3 cups (450 g/1 lb) self-raising
flour

1 teaspoon freshly squeezed
lemon juice

pinch of salt

vegetable or peanut oil
for deep-frying

Greek honey, warmed, to serve

ground cinnamon, to serve

finely chopped toasted
walnuts, to serve

Dissolve yeast in half the warm water. Add caster sugar and vanillin, and whisk together. Add two-thirds of the flour and whisk until smooth. Cover with cling wrap and leave in a warm place for 1 hour.

Add remaining warm water, lemon juice, salt and remaining flour to the batter. Cover again and allow batter to rise until it begins to bubble (about 1½ hours).

Heat oil in a frying pan (or heavy-based saucepan) for deep-frying. Test the oil temperature by dropping in a small piece of bread – if it sizzles, the oil is hot enough. >

Drop tablespoonfuls of mixture into the oil (cook about six at a time). Cook until golden-brown on both sides (about 5–8 minutes), then remove with a slotted spoon and drain on paper towel.

Place doughnuts on a serving plate, drizzle with warm honey, sprinkle with cinnamon and chopped walnuts and serve immediately.

These doughnuts can also be stuffed with ice-cream. When you are ready to fry them, remove ice-cream from freezer so it softens slightly. Cook the doughnuts, then make a slit in each one and place 1 teaspoon ice-cream in the cavity. Serve immediately.

Strava Pastries

Makes about 36

500 g (1 lb 2 oz) plain flour

½ cup (125 ml/4 fl oz) olive oil

½ teaspoon salt

1 cup (250 ml/8½ fl oz) warm
water

250 g butter, melted

NUT FILLING

250 g (9 oz) walnuts,
roughly chopped

250 g (9 oz) almonds,
roughly chopped

½ cup (90 g/3 oz) soft
brown sugar

½ teaspoon ground cinnamon

½ teaspoon ground nutmeg

½ teaspoon ground cloves

LEMON SYRUP

2 cups (440 g/15½ oz) caster
sugar

1 cup (300 g/10½ oz) honey

2 tablespoons (40 ml/1½ fl oz)
freshly squeezed lemon juice

2 strips lemon zest

1 cinnamon stick

Preheat oven to 180°C (360°F). Line a baking tray with baking paper.

In a bowl combine sifted flour with the oil, salt and warm water, mixing until
a dough forms. Turn out onto a clean work surface and knead until dough is
smooth (about 10 minutes). Allow to stand at room temperature for 1 hour.

Combine ingredients for the nut filling and set aside. >

Divide dough into six portions and roll out until very thin (the thinner the better). Brush generously with melted butter. Leaving a 5-mm (¼-in) border, sprinkle a quarter of the nut mixture over each. Roll up each piece of dough to form a log shape. Cut logs, on an angle, into 2.5-cm (1-in) pieces. Place rounds, cut side up, on baking tray and bake in a moderate oven for 45 minutes or until golden-brown.

To make the syrup, add all ingredients to a saucepan with 2 cups (500 ml/ 17 fl oz) water, bring to the boil and simmer for about 10 minutes. Allow to cool.

Remove strava from oven and dip each piece in warm syrup until completely covered. Allow to cool before serving.

Store in an airtight container for up to 2 weeks.

Strava is a Kastellorizian sweet, named after the angle on which it is cut. It is made for special occasions such as name days and weddings.

Easter Bread

Tsoureki

Makes 2 loaves

2 × 7-g (½-oz) packets dried
  rapid-rise yeast

½ teaspoon salt

1 × 10-g (⅜-oz) packet mahlepi

⅓ cup (75 g/2½ oz) caster
  sugar

½ cup (125 ml/4 fl oz) warm
  water

½ cup (125 ml/4 fl oz)
  warm milk

2 tablespoons (40 g/1½ oz)
  butter, melted

1 egg, beaten

3 cups (450 g/1 lb) plain flour

1 egg, beaten

½ cup toasted almond flakes

Preheat oven to 180°C (360°C). Line a baking tray with baking paper and oil lightly.

Place yeast in a mixing bowl, add salt, mahlepi and half the sugar. Whisk in warm water, milk and butter, and leave for 10 minutes. Mix in egg and remaining sugar, then add sifted flour and turn out onto a clean work surface. Knead with your hands until flour is completely combined. If dough is a little sticky, add a little more flour.

Place dough in a clean bowl, cover with a clean tea towel and place in a warm spot for 2 hours or until dough has doubled in size. >

Cut dough in half and divide each half into three, to make 6 portions. Roll each piece into a long snake. Plait three snakes together and place on the prepared tray. Repeat with remaining snakes. Cover with a clean tea towel, place tray in a warm place and let dough rise for 30 minutes or until doubled in size.

Brush the tsoureki with egg and sprinkle with almonds. Bake for 25–30 minutes or until golden-brown. Let cool before serving. Store in an airtight container for up to 1 week.

- Mahlepi is a special spice available at Greek delis.
- Tsoureki is one of the various breads baked during Holy Week in preparation for the traditional midnight supper before or on Easter Sunday. The three dough ropes, plaited together, symbolise the Holy Trinity.

Extras

The secret to Greek cooking can sometimes be found in the special extras. These help enhance the flavours of the fresh produce used in each dish. Dressings give salads and roasted vegetables an added zing, while homemade pastry adds extra flavour to spanakopita. Roasts become even more delicious when a nut stuffing is used and a serving of keftedes gets an extra burst of taste when served with a tomato–chilli chutney.

< Olive Paste (page 232)

Olive Paste

½ cup pistachio nuts

400 g (14 oz) pitted kalamata
  olives

⅓ cup (80 ml/3 fl oz) olive oil

2 tablespoons (40 ml/1½ fl oz)
  freshly squeezed lemon juice

½ teaspoon dried oregano

1 clove garlic, chopped

6 anchovy fillets

2 tablespoons chopped
  fresh parsley

2 tablespoons chopped
  fresh basil

Place all the ingredients in a food processor and blend for about 2 minutes
or until a thick paste forms.

Serve with toasted pita bread.

Homemade Short-crust Pastry Sheets

Makes 500 g (1 lb 2 oz)

500 g (1 lb 2 oz) plain flour
1 teaspoon salt
½ cup (125 ml/4 fl oz) olive oil
½ cup (125 ml/4 fl oz) warm water
2 eggs, beaten

Sift flour and salt into a large bowl. Make a well in the centre and pour in the oil, warm water and eggs. Using your hands, gradually draw the flour from the sides of the well into the liquid. Mix until a dough forms.

Turn dough out onto a clean floured surface and knead lightly until soft and elastic. Place ball of dough into a clean bowl, cover with cling wrap or a clean tea towel and leave to rest for about 1–2 hours.

Place dough on a lightly floured clean surface and roll out into very thin sheets.

Dough should be used immediately, or frozen and thawed when required.

Roasted Garlic, Lemon & Oregano Dressing

Makes about ¾ cup

10 cloves garlic, unpeeled

½ cup (125 ml /4 fl oz) olive oil

**salt and freshly ground
black pepper**

**⅓ cup (80 ml/3 fl oz) freshly
squeezed lemon juice**

½ teaspoon dried oregano

Preheat oven to 200°C (390°F).

Place garlic on a piece of aluminium foil. Drizzle with a little oil and a pinch of salt. Wrap the foil tightly around the garlic, place on a baking tray and roast in the preheated oven until soft (about 20 minutes).

Allow garlic to cool slightly, then remove skins.

Place garlic flesh and remaining ingredients in a food processor, and blend well.

Drizzle dressing over salad or roasted vegetables.

Honey & Mustard Dressing

Makes about ¾ cup

½ cup (125 ml/4 fl oz) olive oil

1 tablespoon Dijon mustard

1 tablespoon Greek honey

2 tablespoons (40 ml/1½ fl oz)
  freshly squeezed lemon juice

1 clove garlic, crushed

Place all ingredients in a screw-top jar and shake vigorously to mix well.

Drizzle dressing over salad of your choice.

Tomato–chilli Chutney

2 kg (4 lb 6 oz) ripe tomatoes,
chopped

2 large onions, chopped
into chunks

3 cloves garlic, finely chopped

1 small red capsicum,
finely chopped

⅓ cup (75 g/2½ oz) firmly
packed soft brown sugar

1 teaspoon dried chilli flakes
(optional)

1 cinnamon stick

1 teaspoon ground allspice

1 teaspoon mustard powder

1 cup (250 ml/8½ fl oz)
red-wine vinegar

salt and freshly ground
black pepper

Put all ingredients in a saucepan over low–medium heat and season to
taste with salt and pepper. Cook, uncovered, for about 45 minutes, stirring
occasionally, until sauce thickens.

Remove chutney from heat and let cool completely. Remove cinnamon
stick and store sauce in a sealed container in the refrigerator until needed.
(It will keep for about 2 weeks.)

This chutney can be served with roasted meats, vegetables or pasta dishes.

Mayonnaise

2 egg yolks

1 tablespoon Dijon mustard

¼ teaspoon sugar

½ teaspoon salt

½ teaspoon white pepper

pinch of cayenne pepper (optional)

3 tablespoons (60 ml/2 fl oz) freshly squeezed lemon juice

1½ cups (375 ml/12½ fl oz) olive oil

In a food processor, beat the egg yolks, mustard, sugar, salt, pepper and cayenne (if using). Add lemon juice and mix well. Slowly drizzle oil drop by drop into the mixture until the sauce begins to thicken. Add the remaining oil in a slow stream, so that the eggs can emulsify with it. (If at any time the mayonnaise splits, add a tablespoon of hot water). Scrape down the sides of the bowl, and keep mixing for about 5 minutes, making sure all the oil has been absorbed. The mayonnaise should look thick creamy and slightly yellow. Season to taste.

You can flavour the mayonnaise by adding 3 tablespoons chopped basil, dill or parsley

Tomato Sauce

Makes 2–3 cups

⅓ cup (80 ml/3 fl oz) olive oil

1 large onion, finely chopped

2 cloves garlic, finely chopped

1 tablespoon dried oregano

salt

800 g (1 lb 12 oz) canned chopped tomatoes

½ cup (125 ml/4 fl oz) white wine

1 tablespoon tomato paste

freshly ground black pepper

about 1 teaspoon sugar

2 tablespoons finely chopped fresh parsley

Heat oil in a heavy-based saucepan over low heat. Add onion and garlic, and sauté until soft. Add dried oregano, ½ teaspoon salt, and cook for about 5 minutes, stirring occasionally. Add tomatoes, white wine and tomato paste, and season to taste with salt, pepper and sugar. Add parsley and simmer, uncovered, for about 20 minutes or until the sauce thickens.

This sauce can be served with pasta, rice or fried potatoes. Store in an airtight container in the fridge for up to 5 days.

Red Capsicum & Tomato Sauce

Makes 4–5 cups

1 kg (2 lb 3 oz) red capsicums

2 kg (4 lb 6 oz) ripe tomatoes, peeled, deseeded and chopped

1 cup (250 ml/8½ fl oz) olive oil

8 cloves garlic, finely chopped

½ leek, finely chopped

2 tablespoons chopped parsley

2 tablespoons chopped basil

1 tablespoon dried oregano

½ teaspoon sugar

salt and freshly ground black pepper

Preheat oven to 200°C (390°F). Line a baking tray with baking paper.

Place capsicums on prepared tray and roast in the oven, turning occasionally, until skins are charred (about 20 minutes). Remove from oven, place in a bowl and cover with cling wrap until cooled. Peel, deseed and chop the flesh into small pieces.

In a large saucepan, combine the tomatoes, oil, garlic, leek and herbs. Simmer over low heat, stirring gently, until most of the liquid has evaporated. Add the capsicum flesh, sugar, and season with salt and pepper. Continue to simmer, stirring occasionally, for 30–40 minutes, or until the sauce has reduced and thickened. Remove sauce from heat and let cool. Transfer sauce to sterilised jars, cover with a layer of oil and seal. Store in the fridge for up to six months. Serve as an accompaniment to sausages, meatballs, grilled meats or fish.

Egg–lemon Cream Sauce

Makes about 2½ cups

**2 tablespoons (40 g/1½ oz)
   butter**

**3 tablespoons (45 g/1½ oz)
   cornflour**

**2 cups (500 ml/17 fl oz)
   hot stock**

3 egg yolks

juice of 1 lemon

Heat butter in a small saucepan over medium heat. When butter has melted, add flour and stir until smooth. Add hot stock and cook over low heat, stirring continuously, until mixture boils. Remove from heat.

In a small bowl beat the egg yolks with the lemon juice. Slowly beat in a few tablespoons of the stock mixture, then add egg–lemon mixture to the stock, stirring continuously. Return saucepan to low heat for 2–3 minutes.

Remove sauce from heat and season with salt and pepper.

This sauce can be served with any meat or poultry dish (using the appropriate stock).

Egg & Lemon Sauce

Salsa avgolemono

Makes about 2 cups

3 eggs

juice of 1–2 lemons

**1½ cups (375 ml/12½ fl oz)
boiling stock**

**salt and freshly ground
black pepper**

In a bowl lightly beat the eggs with the lemon juice. Gradually add the hot stock, whisking continuously to prevent eggs curdling. Season with salt and pepper.

Add this sauce to a soup or stew and gently heat through, stirring until it thickens (do not allow to boil or the sauce will curdle).

- For a lighter and fluffier sauce, separate the eggs and beat the whites until stiff peaks form. Beat yolks and lemon juice into egg whites, then add stock as above.

- Use fish, chicken, beef or vegetable stock, depending on the type of dish you will be using the sauce in.

Grandma Eleni's Rice, Sultana & Pine Nut Stuffing

Makes about 1½ cups

125 g (4½ oz) butter

2 medium-sized onions, chopped

2 cloves garlic, thinly sliced

¾ cup medium-grain rice

½ cup toasted pine nuts

½ cup sultanas

1 teaspoon ground cinnamon

¼ teaspoon ground cloves

½ cup (125 ml/4 fl oz) sweet red wine

1½ cups (375 ml/12½ fl oz) chicken stock

salt and freshly ground black pepper

Heat butter in a saucepan over medium heat, add onion and garlic, increase heat to high and cook, stirring, until onions have a very dark, rich colour – be careful they don't burn. Add rice, nuts, sultanas, spices, red wine and stock, and season with salt and pepper. Bring to the boil, stirring continuously, then reduce heat and simmer for 10 minutes. Turn off heat, cover and set aside for 30 minutes. The rice should be soft and the stuffing a rich brown colour. Check seasoning.

This stuffing can be used for chicken, lamb or vegetables. It can also be served as a side dish.

Bread & Pistachio Stuffing

Makes about 2½ cups

3 tablespoons (60 ml/2 fl oz)
olive oil

1 large red onion,
finely chopped

2 cloves garlic, crushed

170 g (6 oz) butter

2 cups fresh breadcrumbs

1 cup chopped pistachio
nuts, toasted

½ cup sultanas (optional)

½ teaspoon ground cinnamon

½ teaspoon ground cloves

3 tablespoons (60 ml/2 fl oz)
port or sweet wine

salt and freshly ground
black pepper

Heat oil in a frying pan over medium heat, add onion and garlic, and sauté until onion is a rich golden-brown (be sure not to burn it). Add the remaining ingredients, season to taste, and cook for 5 minutes.

This stuffing can be used to stuff chicken, turkey or lamb.

Béchamel Sauce

Makes about 3 cups

120 g (4 oz) butter

1 cup (150 g/5 oz) plain flour

**salt and freshly ground
   black pepper**

**pinch of ground cinnamon
   or nutmeg (optional)**

**3 cups (750 ml/25 fl oz) warm
   milk**

1 egg, beaten

Heat butter in a saucepan over low heat. Add flour, and salt, pepper and cinnamon or nutmeg (if using) to taste. Stir until well blended.

Remove pan from heat, gradually stir in warm milk and return to heat. Cook over low heat, stirring continuously with a whisk, until sauce becomes thick and smooth. Remove from heat, stir in egg and check seasoning.

Special Ingredients

FETTA CHEESE A firm, salty cheese, traditionally made from sheep's or goat's milk. It is sold packed in brine.

FILO PASTRY Paper-thin sheets of pastry, used to make flaky pies and pastries. Usually multiple sheets are layered on top on each other, each brushed with butter. You have to work quickly with this pastry, as it quickly dries out – cover unused portions with cling wrap or a clean damp cloth. It is sold ready-rolled, either fresh or frozen.

GREEK HONEY Greece has some of the best-quality honey in the world owing to the long sunshine periods the country experiences. Greek honey has specific physical and chemical characteristics and comes from thyme, lavender, rosemary, lime trees and orange trees.

HALOUMI CHEESE A firm, salty cheese, traditionally made with a mixture of sheep and goat's milk. It is suitable for grilling or frying due to its high melting point.

HILOPITES Egg noodles made in linguine-sized strips and then cut into small, square pieces.

KATAIFI PASTRY This finely shredded filo dough can be used for sweet or savoury dishes. As with filo sheets, cover unused portions with cling wrap or a damp cloth while you work, to stop it drying out. Kataifi is available from the freezer section of Greek food stores.

KEFALOGRAVIERA CHEESE A hard cheese made from sheep's milk. It has a salty flavour and a rich aroma. It is often used in saganaki and is very similar to kefalotiri.

KEFALOTIRI A very hard textured cheese, it is made with a combination of sheep's and goat's milk and is yellow in colour. It has a very sharp taste, similar to parmesan.

METAXA BRANDY A distilled spirit from Greece, it is a blend of brandy and wine. Metaxa comes in five major varieties: Three Stars, Five Stars, Seven Stars, Twelve Stars and the Grand Reserve with the number of stars representing the number of years the blend is matured.

OKRA Mild-flavoured, slender green vegetable seed pods. When cooked, they release a thick substance that acts as a thickening agent.

VINE LEAVES Leaves of the grape vine, used for wrapping ingredients before cooking. Fresh or brined leaves may be used – if using brined leaves, you'll need to rinse them, then soak them in fresh water for about 20 minutes before use.

Conversions

(Note: all conversions are approximate)

Important note: All cup and spoon measures given in this book are based on Australian standards. The most important thing to remember is that an Australian cup = 250 ml, while an American cup = 237 ml and a British cup = 284 ml. Also, an Australian tablespoon is equivalent to 4 teaspoons, not 3 teaspoons as in the United States and Britain. US equivalents have been provided throughout for all liquid cup/spoon measures. Equivalents for dry ingredients measured in cups/spoons have been included for flour, sugar and rising agents such as baking powder. For other dry ingredients (chopped vegetables, nuts, etc.), American cooks should be generous with their cup measures – slight variations in quantities of such ingredients are unlikely to affect results.

VOLUME

Australian cups/spoons	Millilitres	US fluid ounces
*1 teaspoon	5 ml	
1 tablespoon (4 teaspoons)	20 ml	¾ fl oz
1½ tablespoons	30 ml	1 fl oz
2 tablespoons	40 ml	1½ fl oz
¼ cup	60 ml	2 fl oz
⅓ cup	80 ml	3 fl oz
½ cup	125 ml	4 fl oz
¾ cup	180 ml	6 fl oz
1 cup	250 ml	8½ fl oz
4 cups	1 L	34 fl oz

*the volume of a teaspoon is the same around the world

SIZE

Centimetres	Inches
1 cm	⅜ in
2 cm	¾ in
2.5 cm	1 in
5 cm	2 in
10 cm	4 in
15 cm	6 in
20 cm	8 in
30 cm	12 in

TEMPERATURE

Celsius	Fahrenheit
150°C	300°F
160°C	320°F
170°C	340°F
180°C	360°F
190°C	375°F
200°C	390°F
210°C	410°F
220°C	420°F

WEIGHT

Grams	Ounces
15 g	½ oz
30 g	1 oz
60 g	2 oz
85 g	3 oz
110 g	4 oz
140 g	5 oz
170 g	6 oz
200 g	7 oz
225 g	8 oz (½ lb)
450 g	16 oz (1 lb)
500 g	1 lb 2 oz
900 g	2 lb
1 kg	2 lb 3 oz

Index

PENGUIN BOOKS

Published by the Penguin Group
Penguin Group (Australia)
250 Camberwell Road, Camberwell, Victoria 3124, Australia
(a division of Pearson Australia Group Pty Ltd)
Penguin Group (USA) Inc.
375 Hudson Street, New York, New York 10014, USA
Penguin Group (Canada)
90 Eglinton Avenue East, Suite 700, Toronto, Canada ON M4P 2Y3
(a division of Pearson Penguin Canada Inc.)
Penguin Books Ltd
80 Strand, London WC2R 0RL England
Penguin Ireland
25 St Stephen's Green, Dublin 2, Ireland
(a division of Penguin Books Ltd)
Penguin Books India Pvt Ltd
11 Community Centre, Panchsheel Park, New Delhi – 110 017, India
Penguin Group (NZ)
67 Apollo Drive, Rosedale, North Shore 0632, New Zealand
(a division of Pearson New Zealand Ltd)
Penguin Books (South Africa) (Pty) Ltd
24 Sturdee Avenue, Rosebank, Johannesburg 2196, South Africa

Penguin Books Ltd, Registered Offices: 80 Strand, London, WC2R 0RL, England

First published by Penguin Group (Australia), 2010

10 9 8 7 6 5 4 3 2 1

Text and photographs copyright © Penguin Group (Australia), 2010

The moral right of the author has been asserted

Special thanks to Helen Koutsoukis for the use of her recipes.

Cover design by Claire Tice
Text design by Claire Tice & Marley Flory © Penguin Group (Australia)
Photography by Julie Renouf
Food styling by Lee Blaylock
Typeset in Nimbus Sans Novus by Post Pre-press Group, Brisbane, Queensland
Scanning and separations by Splitting Image P/L, Clayton, Victoria
Printed and bound in China by Everbest Printing Co. Ltd.

National Library of Australia
Cataloguing-in-Publication data:

Kaponis, Yvonne
Greek bible.
ISBN: 9780143202967
Includes index.
1. Cookery, Greek.

641.59495

penguin.com.au